P. L. Travers

Twayne's English Authors Series
Children's Literature

James Gellert, Editor

TEAS 483

P. L. Travers.
Drawing by Eileen Agar.

P. L. Travers

Patricia Demers
University of Alberta

Twayne Publishers • Boston
A Division of G. K. Hall & Co.

P. L. Travers
Patricia Demers

Copyright 1991 by G. K. Hall & Co.
All rights reserved.
Published by Twayne Publishers
A division of G. K. Hall & Co.
70 Lincoln Street
Boston, Massachusetts 02111

Excerpts from *Mary Poppins Opens the Door,* copyright 1943
and renewed 1971 by P. L. Travers, reprinted by permission
of Harcourt Brace Jovanovich, Inc.
Excerpts from *Mary Poppins in the Park,* copyright 1952 and
renewed 1980 by P. L. Travers, reprinted by permission of
Harcourt Brace Jovanovich, Inc.
Excerpts from *About the Sleeping Beauty,* © 1975 by P. L.
Travers, reprinted by permission of Harold Ober Associates,
Incorporated.

Book production by Janet Z. Reynolds.
Typeset by Compset, Inc., Beverly, Massachusetts

First published 1991.
10 9 8 7 6 5 4 3 2 1

The paper used in this publication meets the minimum requirements
of American National Standard for Information Sciences—Permanence
of Paper for Printed Library Materials, ANSI Z39.48-1984. ∞™

Printed and bound in the United States of America.

Library of Congress Cataloging-in-Publication Data

Demers, Patricia, 1946-
    P.L. Travers / Patricia Demers.
      p.   cm. — (Twayne's English authors series ; TEAS 483)
    Includes bibliographical references (p.   ) and index.
    ISBN 0-8057-7005-4
    1. Travers, P. L. (Pamela L.), 1906-   —Criticism and
interpretation.   2. Children's stories, English—History and
criticism.   I. Title.   II. Series.
PR6039.R3Z6   1991
    823′.912—dc20   90-46168
                                                          CIP

Contents

Preface

Although the name P. L. Travers is well known because of her Mary Poppins books, information about her is scarce. Few of her readers know that Travers' professional writing career spans more than six decades and includes fifteen years of theater and film reviewing in London and its environs. The scant critical commentary neglects not only the variety of her accomplishments but the broad scope of the ten books of the Poppins canon itself. Another aspect of her remarkable productivity missed by occasional or piecemeal accounts and reviews is the recognition of her clearly enunciated and largely unchanging views about the omnipresence of myth and fairy tale in our lives, the interconnectedness of all experience and its potential for concord, and the needs of the child who is hidden in each of us.

Before the appearance of *Mary Poppins* in 1934, Travers had established a reputation as a poet, drama critic, and travel essayist in both the *Irish Statesman* and the *New English Weekly*. More mythical than pastoral, her poetry in these periodicals explores the young artist's pursuit of invention as well as the young woman's search for love. Many of the cosmic backdrops of her poems, particularly that of "Zodiac Circus," continue to appear in the Poppins books. The theater criticism, too, forecasts significant themes adumbrated in the Poppins books and throughout the whole of her writing. Just as Travers sees drama as a great continuum stretching from morality plays to barn shows and musicals, she sees literature as an imaginative unity, making no trivializing distinctions between material for adults and for children. She disdains sentimentality, cleverness, and preachiness, and prizes honesty, simplicity, and a genuine exuberance that can border on zaniness. In her theater reviews she values above all

emotional engagement and fidelity to human beings, who must
be more than coat-hangers for ideas. Her standards are not im-
possibly high, yet, without ever succumbing to a strident, intem-
perate tone, she openly denounces failures. These reviews are so
witty, energetic, and clear-sighted that it comes as no revelation
that they are the work of the woman who wrote *Mary Poppins.*

Travers is reluctant to be called the creator of Mary Poppins;
on the contrary, she considers herself open to this unique nanny's
influences and dependent on her visitations. Judging from the
publication of *Mary Poppins and the House Next Door* in 1988,
these happily continue to occur after more than five decades. Dis-
counting the extraordinary and pooh-poohing the fantastic, Mary
Poppins, the prim shapeshifter, partakes of a mythically alive
universe at the same time that she capably manages the domestic
reality of 17 Cherry Tree Lane. Although she is a temporary, literally floating, member of a London household securely locked in
the 1930s, her lineage, which some readers have traced to the
Hindu Terrible Mother, Kali, and others to the goddesses Artemis
and Sophia, is indeed ancient. Yet many of Mary Poppins' man-
nerisms, phrases, and friends are derived, by the author's own
admission, from experiences in Travers' Australian childhood.

As a wartime evacuee living in the United States from 1940 to
1945, Travers turned again to memories of her childhood, in the
form of privately printed gift books, to stave off homesickness and
nurse hopes of reconciliation and peace. As always with Travers,
it is the child's view of the separation and destruction of war that
is most telling. In a diary account written in the voice of an
eleven-year-old girl evacuated to America, *I Go by Sea, I Go by
Land,* and in children's comments on the Christmas Eve carol service held at St. Paul's Cathedral in 1945, recounted in *The Fox at
the Manger,* Travers offers tentative constructs of unity and concord to bridge differences of geography and attitude.

Travers' retellings, lectures, and essays, especially her recent
and regular contributions to *Parabola: The Magazine of Myth and
Tradition,* pursue the issue of connectedness by examining some
of the ways in which the past impinges upon and continually influences the present. *Friend Monkey,* a reshaping of the Hanu-

man legend from the Ramayana, places an overzealous but always likable monkey in the London of Victoria's Diamond Jubilee, where his good intentions wreak havoc. *About the Sleeping Beauty* not only relates the fairy tale in a distinctly Jungian mode but also theorizes about the awakening involved in each individual's development. As my meeting and conversation with P. L. Travers in June 1988 confirmed, her concern for understanding as a never-ending quest, which frequently relies on the undervalued forms of fairy tale and legend to convey subtle messages, remains for me the hallmark of her extensive writing career. It is both curious and apposite that an author who takes such pains to conceal biographical data should be so fully, consistently, and humanely revealed in her work.

Patricia Demers

University of Alberta

Acknowledgments

Thinking is linking, as Travers asserts, and so, by extension, is writing. I wish to thank the people who have encouraged and assisted my attempts to assemble this study. I am grateful to Lois Kuznets and Jon Stott for offering me the project, to P. L. Travers for so graciously consenting to an interview, and to James Gellert for editing so instructively. A Faculty of Arts travel grant helped to start the research in London, where the staff at the Colindale Branch of the British Library was especially obliging. Particular thanks for unearthing material or setting me in the right direction are due to Marilyn Atkins and John Chalmers of the Harry Ransom Humanities Research Center at the University of Texas at Austin; Julie Baldwin of Collins Publishers; Valerie Baynton, Curator of the Sir Henry Doulton Gallery at Stoke-on-Trent; Martha Cox of the Archives Department of Theodore Presser Music Publishers; Susan Reiss of the New York Parks Commission in the Arsenal at Central Park; Christine Salmon of the University of London; and Dr. Rebecca Stafford, President of Chatham College in Pittsburgh.

P. L. Travers has permitted me to use all the material quoted in the text and appendix, and I take this opportunity to thank her for her kindness.

Chronology

1965 Writer in residence, Radcliffe College, Cambridge, Massachusetts.

1966 Writer in residence, Smith College, Northampton, Massachusetts.

1968 *Maria Poppina ab A ad Z.*

1969 *A Mary Poppins Story for Coloring.*

1970 Clark lecturer, Scripps College, Claremont, California: "In Search of the Hero."

1971 *Friend Monkey.*

1973 *George Ivanovitch Gurdjieff.*

1975 *About the Sleeping Beauty* and *Mary Poppins in the Kitchen; A Cookery Book with a Story.*

1976 Becomes consulting editor and regular contributor to *Parabola.*

1977 Awarded the Order of the British Empire.

1978 Awarded honorary doctorate of humane letters at Chatham College, Pittsburgh, Pennsylvania; participates in symposium on the Celtic consciousness at the University of Toronto.

1980 *Two Pairs of Shoes.*

1981 *Mary Poppins* (revised edition).

1982 *Mary Poppins in Cherry Tree Lane.*

1988 *Mary Poppins and the House Next Door.*

1989 *What the Bee Knows.*

1

A Writer's Life:
Seeking and Finding

An unapologetic "traditionalist," Pamela Lyndon Travers prefers to "begin at the beginning."[1] For readers of contemporary autobiography who are accustomed to the idea of a walking text and a notion of the self that is only as convincing as its last construction, there is a comforting stability in such a statement. But the scant detail available about Travers' own beginning—her Australian childhood; the influence of parents, nannies, and household employees; and her early addiction to writing and acting—creates a mere illusion of facticity. These few glimpses of childhood, based on occasional remarks and rare disclosures, come from a woman who has described herself as "a very private person" and "rather shy of publicity," which "pulls me out of my socket."[2] She has been just as forthright yet flummoxing with other interviewers. For Joseph Roddy she held forth on one of her favorite topics, not writing for children: "I don't write for children at all. I turn my back on them."[3] Her answer to the repeated questions, "where did she come from?" and "why did she go?," is both candid and oblique: "the idea of Mary Poppins has been blowing in and out of me, like a curtain at a window, all my life."[4] Although her writing emerges "from the hodgepodge of living," Travers likes to keep the process of creation "dark" and "entirely spontaneous, . . . not thought out."[5] Moreover, she is categorical about an author's works being the only criterion of assessment, doubting, as she

1

confided in Jonathan Cott, "that biographies are of any use at
all."[6] This dismissal of biographical data probably owes as much
to Travers' aversion to analysis, which she views as a post mor-
tem on the literary cadaver, as to her disagreement with the biog-
rapher's penchant for compartments, stages, and categories.
Because she has maintained an openness to the events and sensations, joyful and sorrowful, of her own childhood, she can assert
that "the ideas I had then move about in me now" and that "sorrow lies like a heartbeat behind everything I have written."[7]
Hence, "beginning at the beginning" for an author who wishes to
be called anonymous, who finds explanations unnecessary, who
considers herself more of a listener than a writer, and who refuses
to write for children is more difficult than it first appears. If, however, one is willing to believe in "radical innocence," a term Travers borrows from Yeats to convey an adult's linking "by some thin
spider thread" to her youth, and to take "time . . . into timelessness . . . long before the flyleaf and long after the back
page,"[8] then Travers' life displays this sense of continuity and
integration.

Born in Queensland, the eldest of three children of Robert and
Margaret (Goff) Travers, she grew up in a home drenched in the
Celtic twilight. Her Irish father, lyrical and melancholy, amiable
and opinionated, was a sugar planter who had first planted tea
in Ceylon after leaving Ireland. Her Australian-born mother, of
Scottish and Irish descent, contributed to the family's consciousness of things Irish by hiring a succession of Irish nannies. Her
father's visits to the nursery and his lilting tenor would cause the
composure of one of the stone-hearted nannies to dissolve "as
swiftly as sugar in tea."[9] "Argumentative" as well, he was more
willing than his wife to grapple with young Pamela's queries, especially after she had been let loose on the Bible. More than six
decades later, Travers was to recreate this exchange, which reflects both the perplexity of the father and the tenacity of the
child.

> "Father," I said to the back of the newspaper, "what is
> a concubine?"

"Er-hum," he murmured, playing for time. "Why on earth do you ask?"

"Well, it says in the Bible that David got him more concubines and Solomon had four hundred."

"Well," he said reasonably. "David and Solomon were heads of the house and they needed someone to look after them and the concubines—er—did."

"What a pity, Father, you have only two!"

"Two what?" Having answered the question he had lost interest.

"Two concubines—Katie and Bella to cook and clean?"

"Katie and Bella are not my concubines." He was manifestly put out.

"Then—Nelly?" Nelly was simple-minded and helped with the washing.

"Certainly not!"

"Then, Father, who *are* your concubines?"

"I have no concubines!" he roared and flung the newspaper at me.

The head of the house and no concubines! How low he must be on the social scale![10]

Although her mother might announce impromptu breakfast picnics several miles from home and serve supper spread out on the floor, there were nonetheless moments of undisguised tension with her first child. One of these occasions, set in the nursery, involved her mother "being daintily, fiercely cross" while she tidied up and put the toys away in the cupboard. While her daughter sat on the bed and watched, the woman tossed the child's beloved china-faced doll at the bed "with a ferocious gesture," commanding, "'Put it away yourself!'" In the ensuing scene, her mother touchingly replaces anger with penitence.

I put out my arms a moment too late, and the doll's face struck the iron frame and shattered to smithereens.

"Mother, you've killed her!" I cried in despair—feeling the crack in my own body.

My mother sat down and wept. Her tears fell slowly
into her lap. She picked up the broken china pieces and
cradled the body in her arms. "Forgive me, forgive me,"
she said to the doll, but I knew she was speaking to me.
All my life I remembered this scene. She was grieving,
and even then I somehow knew it, not merely for the
broken doll, but because she had hurt her child.[11]

Far removed from Kenneth Grahame's dragonish Olympians,
Travers' parents were neither insensitive nor particularly intru-
sive in their children's lives. Her recollections, as one of "the
lumps in the family porridge," are very fond and discerning, evok-
ing "an atmosphere in which tradition was still part of life, laws
few, fixed and simple, and children taken for granted."[12] She and
her siblings were treated as neither equals nor prodigies. No
great fuss was made about her writing, producing, or acting in
school plays. In retrospect Travers applauds this indifference as
"the most sensible way to treat the budding artist" and expresses
thanks that her talent was not "doused into nothingness by
friendly praise."[13] An accusatory insolence, however, associated
with the outsider or the isolate, creeps into Travers' picture of a
mother and father, who were often preoccupied with other things.
"I used to look at my parents and think silently, 'You amaze me!
You've learned so much, you've lived so long; and yet you don't
hear, you can't answer my questions, you can never, never enlighten me.'"[14]

But enlightenment came, in a sense unbidden and impercepti-
ble, through all the distinctive forms of her subtropical locale.
Even as a child she "could sense the antiquity" of the land.[15] Her
memories of chewing ripe sugar cane, of nesting like a bird in the
tall grasses and weeds, and of spending afternoons rambling
amid the vines and jacaranda trees inform her early poems,
dreams, and play-acting. Growing up in the country, she de-
lighted in making miniature city parks and "took an inward pleasure from making those people" who populated them. Every child,
in Travers' estimate, is "underprivileged in some way." Her own
impoverishment in never having seen a park was cured tempo-

rarily by this pastime, comparable with Jane Banks's designing of the idyllic Park for Poor People. "Something in those parks assuaged something in me—unknown, perhaps, but deeply true. . . . There would I be working on my park until I see a huge grown-up foot crashing through."[16]

Many parallels can be drawn between Travers' childhood and the Poppins books. Her parents offered explanations for nothing. "It was clear from their general attitude," she recalls, "that our parents had no very high opinion of our intelligence, but at the same time, apparently, they expected us to know everything."[17] As well as using "spit-spot into bed" as a habitual phrase, Mrs. Travers actually purchased Mary Poppins' cherished book, *Everything a Lady Should Know,* and consulted it as if it were an "oracle".[18] Among the memorable nannies assigned to the Travers children was the stern Katie Nanna, with her "layers of crackling aprons and always smelling of oatmeal." Katie Nanna's main feature was intransigence: "her ideas on the upbringing of children were as unbending as her aprons and as constant as the fixed stars." The children's veneration is clear, though, in their fanciful image of the nanny's life after she left to marry a fireman. "For, as they imagined it, he took her to live with him on his engine and they pictured the two of them, Paddy Carew very black with soot and Katie Nanna very white with starch, forever talking and making cups of tea on the top of the coal truck."[19] Another nanny, Bella or Bertha, had a parrot-headed umbrella, which she wrapped ceremoniously in tissue paper upon her return from outings. One early prototype of Mrs. Corry's alimentary wonders could have been Nanny Belle's (another nanny) aunt who "Lived on Her Capital"; through synecdochical reasoning the young Travers "saw her gnawing and nibbling bits of her person—her finger, her elbow, her toe—for sustenance."[20] Moreover, real life equivalents existed for many of the animals, characters, and objects in the Poppins books.

> Most of the animals are true. Andrew belonged to my great aunt who, like Miss Lark, pampered him and made him a nincompoop. Pompey, the dachshund, owned by

Admiral Boom in the books, sits by me as I write, and
Princess Crocus, the tortoiseshell cat in "Lucky Thursday," has just had her fiftieth kitten. "The Cat that
Looked at a King," in the chapter of that name, stares
down at me now from the mantelpiece with his wild
green china eyes. Mrs. Corry, too, really existed. She and
those great sad daughters kept the general store in our
country town. It was frightening as well as exciting to go
inside the little dark shop, for one never knew what her
mood would be. All went well if she was cheerful. If not,
a request for chocolate could easily produce licorice or
even a bar of soap.[21]

Though she describes herself as "a passionately lazy child,"
Travers admits she "ate" her way, "like a bookworm," through the
family library.[22] Like the children's toys, the books were few and
predictable: Scott, Dickens, Shakespeare, Tennyson, Yeats and
other Irish poets, the Grimms, and the Bible. The children's books
were even fewer: Beatrix Potter, E. Nesbit, Ethel Turner, Lewis
Carroll, Charles Kingsley (his *Heroes* gave "the myths straight"),
George Farrow (whose *The Wallypug of Why* is full of fantastic
transformations and journeys), and an assortment of raggedy
penny books. She still remembers the special thrill of dipping into
the not-entirely-understood world of her mother's romantic novels
and her father's grisly *Deathbed Scenes*.

The lifelong repercussions of this voracious and unmonitored
reading have been the subject of some of Travers' most effective
essays. Echoing Joyce's claim that his childhood bent beside him,
Travers attributes her own search for the "inner kingdom [of]
'Happy Ever After'" to the "sturdy toughness" of this reading,
where "the story is there for entertainment and the secrets are
implicit in it," where "Now . . . tell[s] you what happens and . . .
Then . . . bring[s] you back to learn the meaning of it."[23] Clearly
the books of paramount importance were the fairy tales and the
Bible. In her 1944 review for the *New Republic*, she hailed the
Hunt and Stern translation of Grimm's Fairy Tales as "a residual
drop of sweetness for children and grown-ups . . . [in] this bitter

year." Not infected with "the virus of humanitarianism" and less cruel than the "artificial grievings of Hans Andersen," the old Marchen are for Travers the reviewer, "our only way to self-awareness," where we may "wrestle with the angel and not loose him till he blesses."[24] She embraces Esau, the Prodigal Son, Ishmael, the Wicked Fairy, Alcott's Dan, and Potter's Peter Rabbit as her "best-loved friends." She sees "the uncompromising black and white of the fairy tales" and the villainies and deceits in biblical narratives as the beginning of her own battle with the cruel, bloody, and tribal features of life. "Somewhere, I thought, in my childishness, there is a place between North and South, where all opposing brothers meet, where black and white meet, where black and white sheep lie down together, where St. George has no enmity to the dragon and the dragon agrees to be slain."[25] Yet, paradoxical as it may seem, Travers prizes most highly the unselfconsciousness of this formative and informing writing. It is an art she illustrates succinctly in this fable. "Once, in a wood, in the early morning, I saw a fox dancing alone just at the edge of a clearing, up and down on his hind legs, swinging his brush in the sun. There was no vixen near, the birds were not interested, nobody in the world cared—he was doing it for his own pleasure. Perhaps most writers are really foxes, dancing their own particular dance without any thought of a watching eye."[26]

Travers' life changed dramatically with the sudden death of her father when she was seven years old. The family moved hundreds of miles south to New South Wales, about twenty miles beyond Sydney, to live with her maternal great-aunt, Christina Saraset. She attended a local grammar school and, at ten, was sent to a boarding school, where she was chosen to play Bottom in a professional production of *A Midsummer Night's Dream*. Although the director was keen on her talent and offered to train her for the stage, Travers' family balked at the idea. "This was quite impossible," she related to Roy Newquist, "in my kind of family at that time."[27] The scraps of information about her teenage life in Australia suggest that saddening responsibilities were placed on her as the widow's eldest child. Rather than accept a scholarship to the University of Sydney, she worked as a cashier for the Australian Gas and Light Company, as a dressmaker, and as a dancer in an Army show. She has admitted somewhat ruefully to Michele Field, "I was brought up from the time my father died, with everybody saying, 'What are you going to do when you grow up to help your mother?'"[28] Significantly, Travers dedicated *Mary Poppins* to her mother, who died at the age of fifty-three, six years before its publication. By the time she was eighteen, Travers had worked as a reporter and as an actress in Australia, before traveling to England in 1924. The search for dates, specific productions, and employers, however, is invariably abortive. Such questions trespass the boundaries Travers has so clearly demarcated between public and private. In coming dangerously close to requests for explanations, they also prompt this "private person" to lift the drawbridge.

What can be pieced together of her early period in London suggests more serendipity than strategic planning. She found work as a reporter, had poetry published in the *Irish Statesman,* and was befriended by its editor, AE (George Russell), whom she met during one of her visits to relatives in Ireland. She met W. B. Yeats and established a reputation as a drama critic and travel essayist in the London-based *New English Weekly* before the first Poppins book appeared in 1934. Typical of the pluck and impulsiveness of the young Travers is her account of the meeting with Yeats. She set out for Lough Gill and Innisfree in the midst of a rainstorm and journeyed back to Dublin by train. With arms laden with rowan branches, looking like a slightly crazed dryad, she presented herself to the poet whom her father had most idolized. To her surprise she was eventually ushered in to his study. While the great man spoke of his poetry, the young aspirant noticed a single sprig of fruiting rowan in a vase. She grasped the point immediately: "The secret is to say less than you need. You don't want a forest, a leaf will do."[29] AE (1867–1935) was both mentor and kindred spirit as well as poet, playwright, painter, theosophist, economist, and revivalist. Travers became a regular visitor to his office at Merrion Square and his home at 17 Rathgar Avenue. AE was attached to the Eastern Scriptures and Celtic heroes and saw Travers "as daughter, acolyte, apprentice, or as all three." He not only fished up friends for her "from his inexhaustible cauldron"[30] but also taught her precious lessons by example. From AE she learned of the "unknown comrades in many moods, whose naked souls pass through ours and reveal themselves to us in an unforgettable instant." She also heard about a vow of true poverty, which makes one "ready at any time to desert prosperity or fame if these conflict with the spirit."[31] It is tempting and, in fact, fitting to see traces of his influence everywhere in Travers' work. According to AE's criteria in his "Essay on the Character in Irish Literature," her writing appears to be inherently Irish, absorbed in "poetic or spiritual truth, a relation of myth and image to deep inner being." For AE the Irish imagination is not philosophic but visionary, with every vision being "what it seems at the moment to the seer."[32] His comments on Mary Poppins, whom he called "Popkins" and whom he described as a possible manifestation of the Hindu goddess Kali, are often cited. It can be argued that Travers' whole career is a form of tribute to or working out of AE's ideas. Her intuitive trust in the perceptions of childhood echoes AE's joy at recapturing his lost wonder world, which he described in "What Home" from *The House of the Titans* (1934):

> O, how I wreaked my childhood's spite
> When I first dwindled to this day,
> Thinking on my lost wonder world
> That was so very far away.
>
> And now my heart has come to rest,
> Or the green earth has homelier grown.
> Its children creep into my heart,
> Woodland and water, hill and stone.[33]

Travers' current essays in *Parabola* all concern "The Vesture of the Soul," a poem by AE, whose treatment of the "tattered dress . . . patched and stained with dust and rain" and "the viewless spirit's wide domain" provides a preview, fifty years earlier, of such tales as "Speak, Lord" (7.2.1982), "The Way Back" (9.3.1984), "The Garment" (10.4.1985) and "Le Chevalier Perdu" (12.1.1987).

In Travers' career serendipity appears to play a great role, while exact chronology remains elusive. Before her trip to Russia (the subject of *Moscow Excursion*) and during her recuperation from a serious but undisclosed illness, Travers began relating some of Mary Poppins' escapades to two children. At the time she was living in the thatched Sussex cottage mentioned in *The Doomsday Book* as "The Pound House". It seems appropriate that the combination of ancient surroundings and a youthful audience should have instigated storytelling comparable with the sort with which she had regaled her siblings in the old-young land of Australia. Hendrik van Loon, the popularizer of historical subjects, drew to her attention the real curiosity of the book, not how she thought of Mary Poppins but "how Mary Poppins came to think of [her]." Travers' own assessment of the creative process is equally mysterious: "I think that Mary Poppins just fell into me at a time when I was particularly open."[34] She worked as a drama critic for the *New English Weekly* until the outbreak of the war, at which time she decided to leave England for America, at the request of the British Ministry of Education. While abroad, she published *I Go by Sea, I Go by Land,* an account of the evacuation to the United States told from the point of view of an eleven-year-old girl and the third of the Mary Poppins books. Travers also sent back "Letters from Another World" for the *New English Weekly*. To cope with her homesickness she accepted the invitation of a friend, John Collier, administrator for Indian Affairs, to travel west and stay on several Navaho, Hopi, and Pueblo reservations. The effect was salutary: she talked to and rode with the Indians, joined their dances, and was rewarded with a secret Pueblo name. This gesture, as she confided to Edwina Burness and Jerry Griswold, was extremely moving because she has "a strong feeling about names, that names are a part of a person, a very private thing to each one."[35] Her return to England at the end of the war, as her column in the *New English Weekly* and the fable *The Fox at the Manger* indicate, signaled a slow return to normalcy or, more accurately, a reacquaintance with a ravaged country building anew.

Travers' lectures, interviews, and essays, along with the additional Poppins books, the full-length story of the Hanuman figure, *Friend Monkey,* and the retelling of and psychological meditation on the fairy tale *About the Sleeping Beauty,* show the cohesiveness of her views and, more remarkably, her immense productivity into her seventies and eighties. The fourth Poppins book, *Mary Poppins in the Park,* is one of the author's favorites: six finely crafted stories, more Platonic than whimsical, all concerned with the world of the interior and the seamless unity linking illusion and reality. *Mary Poppins from A to Z, Maria Poppina ab A ad Z, A Mary Poppins Story for Coloring,* and *Mary Poppins in the Kitchen* are a series of witty jokes and diversions, just slightly more high-minded than spin-offs. But the two latest books, *Mary Poppins in Cherry Tree Lane* and *Mary Poppins and the House Next Door,* are clear returns to myth and fairy tale, stressing the possibilities of concord, harmony, and the unification of past and present, child and adult, vision and actuality. Although the trivializing Disney movie secured a whole new generation of Mary Poppins fans, Travers' work addresses themes that deny special pleading or, what she considers worse, meretricious simplifying and sanitizing for children.

Part of Travers' subversive activity is to question accepted ideas. The folly of viewing childhood and adulthood as hermetically sealed categories is one of her recurring themes. As writer-in-residence at Smith College, Northampton, Massachusetts, in 1966, she tried to convince students that education is not "collected knowledge" but "thinking and listening"; as she later confessed in a lecture at Scripps College in Claremont, California, she is proud of being "an anarchist as regards education."[36] One label she disagrees with strenuously is "literature for children," maintaining that it is "hard both on children and on literature." She delights in having "no idea where childhood ends and maturity begins" and prefers to see the author as a "necessary lunatic who remains attentive and in readiness, unselfconscious,

unconcerned, all disbelief suspended—even when frogs turn into princes and nursemaids, against all gravity, slide up the
bannisters."[37]

Understandably, P. L. Travers' current work in *Parabola* is one
aspect of her own idiosyncratic quest for meaning. It reveals the
influences of Zen Buddhism and the gnosticism of the Russian
emigré George Ivanovitch Gurdjieff, and reflects the tutelage of
one of her more contemporary mentors, Karlfried Graf Dürckheim. Both Gurdjieff's "kind of unravelling" that is "not so much
a discovering as an uncovering of secret things" and Dürckheim's
call to "remain the children of Life—Life that reveals itself in
everlasting change"[38] are signposts in Travers' journey back
through her past, a journey in which she attempts to take time
into timelessness.

2

Apprenticeship as a Poet: "Too much fire for a time that has grown cold"

We have need of the beauty
In songs sung and words spoken
Out of the sorrowing heart.
—"Oh, Break Her Heart,"
Irish Statesman, 5 June 1926

The smattering of poems (fourteen in the *Irish Statesman* and eight in the *New English Weekly*) and essays (five in the *Irish Statesman*), which Travers wrote early in her career (1926–37), establishes her as neither primarily a poet nor an essayist. Although full of the joys and sorrows of love, her poems are more than mere amateur verses. Often possessed of an elfin charm, Travers' poems may manoeuvre ironic curves or keen with a cosmic grief at love gone wrong. They are rich in potent, and at times vertiginous, metaphors, which foreshadow many of the themes she explored in a lifetime of writing. Among these are the search for reconciliation, the participation in a mythically alive universe, and the openness to emotional attachments, all of which present the author as intuitive and vulnerable, yet hidden.

In whatever way they are coaxed or teased from the writing, these deductions ultimately reveal the difficulty of knowing the author. It is important, however, to weigh this conclusion very carefully since Travers has insisted that she be known only through her work and has taken pains to conceal biographical

13

information. Although the text is imprinted with a strong sense
of personality and current theoretical writings[1] challenge many
of the distinctions between public and private, essential differences between the work and the life remain. In *Search for a
Method* Jean-Paul Sartre describes the life as "illuminated by the
work as a reality whose total determination is found outside of it,
both in the conditions that bring it about and in the artistic creation that realizes it and finishes it off by expressing it." For
Sartre, the work "as the objectification of the person is, in fact,
more complete, more total than the life," but despite its useful-
ness in being "a research tool to clarify the biography, . . . the
work *never* reveals the secrets of the biography."[2] Roland Barthes
theorizes that reflections of personality and life upon language
and writing are elusive, involving the dialectic of affirmation and
negation, but resulting only in desubstantification—the loss of
solidity or essence. In Julia Kristeva's comments on Barthes'
Writing Degree Zero and *S/Z*, writing for Barthes absorbs the neg-
ative mode "into a semblance of affirmation (the moment of in-
scription), but only a semblance, because what is inscribed is
always already broken up within the ungraspable, impersonal,
transsubjective, anonymous, musical plurality of the . . . text."[3]
Kristeva concludes that "it is henceforth naive, if not impossible,
to try to generalize from the seesaw motion linking biography and
works."[4]

Such considerations are especially applicable to Travers' early
life and writing. Trying to take into account most of these caveats
about the stability and self-reflexivity of meaning, I therefore pro-
pose to look at Travers' first publications in three stages: her
early poetry in the *Irish Statesman* (1925–28), her essays in that
journal (1929–30), and her occasional poetry in the *New English
Weekly* (1933–37).

Travers' first submissions to the *Irish Statesman* were varia-
tions on pastoral themes, invoking the muses of forest, moor, and
plain to assist her song. At times her own poetic stance is impish;
at others it is mournful. But throughout she is absorbed with the
professional, writerly pursuits of invention and theme-finding. In
"Christopher" (4 April 1925), she is the proud culprit, or "song's

thief," who has stolen "the sylvan note / Searing and high / Out of the linnet's throat / where songs of poets float." She admits to the theft on account of her "need of Christopher," the "linnet-child, / Fay born of fay" who could be a companion, muse, or sibling.

> And I stole her sweetest joy
> Out of the air,
> Made myself a changeling toy
> A little faery-human boy,
> Made him of a brown bird's joy
> What do I care?

Her mood is less casual and more tentative in "The Coming" (18 July 1925), which also concerns the writer's search for invention. Having "flung the thread of a dream / To catch the minnows of silence," she awaits the arrival of "the unseen playmate." "Clad in the lovely skin / Of leopards, sloe flowers in his hair," this Pan-like tutor, whose "mouth is grave and sowed / With the seeds of song," makes her "name silver on the silver air."

The world of these early poems is essentially lyrical. "Te Deum of a Lark" (7 November 1925) is actually a celebration of the bird's "power to ease / [its] heart of pain / in singing, and so / find joy again." The lyricism is not always tame and hymnal: "Happy Sleeping" (27 March 1926) explores the time when the sleeping poet forsakes soft rest and goes

> Where wind in green bough laces
> Wild song, and the gods shake
> Music from trees and wings
> In the wild places.

The "flaming green delight" of her dreams is confirmed by tokens which, though more imagistic than ocular proof, are reminiscent of the corroborative souvenirs in the Mary Poppins books.

> I have awaked to find
> my wrists and ankles bound

> With flushed flowers of eglantine
> Faster than rope could bind,
> And once upon my pillow
> Close to my brow I found
> Rue newly plucked, and nine
> Green wands of willow.

This green world furnishes the poet with topoi and stories, riches she hoards but, in "Oh, Break Her Heart" (5 June 1926), is forced to share. The emphatic single-line refrain, "Oh, break her heart, they said" refers to society, which simultaneously monitors and hungers for her song. No longer will her heart be allowed to "spend its days / Tuliping the woods of love, / Chiming in green loveways." "Breaking the heart" has a double meaning: the predictable disappointing of her girlish expectations and the artistic call to share the beauty of this sorrow. The first connotation involves loss, while the second suggests that rupture and spillage are actually gifts for readers as well as for the artist.

> So that its hoarded honey
> May gild a harper's string,
> Sweet honey and bitter honey
> Spilt for our garnering.
> Let not her heart's wild bees
> Make shining, secret mead
> But from her grief distil
> Loveliness for our need,
> She has an orchard there
> Where the white breast begins
> To blossom—pluck its apples now,
> Unsheathe the javelins!

Though her "lovely rivers" are "loosed from their tides . . . into the mould of a song," and her heart is broken so that its "jasmine words / And rue-green words that weep" are sprayed like a fountain, the emphasis is on creative gains all round.

One of the remarkable features of Travers' early poems is the ways in which she gradually introduces erotic elements into the pastoral world. Her sonnet "Ghost of Two Sad Lovers" (9 October 1926) moves deftly from histrionic immaturity to elegiac grief. Sorrow, having been courted, arrives with a drowning weight until the lovers' story itself is finally swept away:

> Before we knew of grief we longed for grief,
> Spilt tears and bade all contemplate with ruth
> A tragic maiden and a fair sad youth
> Plucking the greenest bough from sorrow's sheaf.
>
> But rue's a heavy garland for the brows
> Fashioned for little joys and we were drowned
> Deep in our lovely folly having found
> Dead leaves may not be blown into a rose—
>
> Never again shall sudden crimson birds
> Light on our cheeks; nor laughter's little doves
> Nest in our mouths; no longer shall we pass
> Imprinting warm foot-shapes upon crisp grass,
> And the sweet broken story of our loves
> Is lost beneath a wind of living words.

In contrast to this loss of story is the desire in "The Dark Fortnight" (29 January 1927) to find a love theme "in this blind, barren time," when "There is no more to be said / Of battles, gallimaufries, kings, / Love feasting on starry bread / Or love, crying with bitter cry." Assisted by equipment drawn from proverbial expressions, the poet then resolves to seek inspiration (or, lactation, as it might be called here) in a process at once natural and figurative:

> I will go find me a spear
> Of wild-goose-feather wrought,
> And fashion the ears of a hare

> To a parchment of silk,
> And pray to the ewes of thought
> To let down their milk.

As a woman I am struck by how Travers' erotic poems (the remainder of her submissions to the *Irish Statesman* and most of those in the *New English Weekly*), both reflect and often confound current feminist thought about what Josepine Donovan calls "the cultural and social expressions of women speaking about their experience and practice, in a woman-grounded epistemology."[5] Of course, Travers' writing, while not prudish, is relatively opaque. Unlike the modernism of such contemporaries as H. D. (Hilda Doolittle) or Virginia Woolf, it floats between the breezy independence, both emotional and sexual, of Edna St. Vincent Millay, and the sardonic humor of Edith Sitwell. Moreover, it rarely fulfills those "structural conditions" which for Donovan characterize "a woman's poetics." Among these shared experiences are the "condition of oppression," the confinement to "the domestic or private sphere," the creation of "objects for use, rather than exchange," "certain physiological experiences" (most universally menstruation), "the childrearing role," and the "gender personality traits . . . [of] interdependency and emotional intensity."[6] It may seem curious that, while her most famous literary character is intricately linked with childrearing, Travers' poetry avoids mentioning this role, concentrating on the domestic sphere or laying stress on the creation of objects for use. Although her poetry about love and its discontents does not tally with many specified gynocritical concerns, it nonetheless provides a great deal more than what Lawrence Lipking has deemed the single plaintive note of women's poetics: "the unsatisfied craving of children who cry to be held."[7] Nina Auerbach's refutation, that women's writing often expresses "the will-to-satisfaction of adults who refuse to be held, and who try to swallow the world that holds us,"[8] more appropriately summarizes the passion, humiliation, and determination of Travers' poetry.

For Travers a certain clearsightedness emerges from periods of disillusionment and dejection. In "The Plane Tree" (23 April

1927), she compares the lush foliage of summer and the bare trees of winter to the philandering blandishments and exposed deceits of a lover. The opening line sets in motion the accusatory tone: "All the summer you have deceived me." The "green insincerity" of the leaves and the meek bending of the branches before the wind convey the wounding implications of this deceit for the "lovesick" poet. At last able to see through the "green falsehood and gold disguise," she bids farewell to the tree (and the lover) in a mood that is as deeply unsettled as it is grimly determined; distinguishing herself from "all" those "drowned" or "drugged" by the glamor of the tree's shade, she declares:

> All save one. I felt your pitiful tides
> Of soft pretence surge at my heart,
> But the long lapping honied urge
> Broke there and drifted aimlessly away.
>
> I knew you then under the dappled shift
> Of leaves stitched through with sunlight,
> Naked and lonely, uncontrite,
> Hiding your sword beneath a farthingale.
>
> I know you now. Winter has laid you bare
> Of green falsehood and gold disguise.
> Farewell the traitor leaves and the soft drone
> Of cozening branches lying to the wind.
>
> Wild, wild and desperate even as I,
> Stark tragic arms beating at heedless heaven
> Hungry for forests and the pathless places
> Our feet set endlessly in trim bleak ways.

More consequences of this disillusionment along with a bourgeoning sense of revival and purposiveness are evident in "No More Eagles" (9 July 1927). Realizing that she has "too much fire / for a time that has grown cold," she determines to persevere:

> And the furious heart
> burns in a gap of silence
> like Spring reddening
> in the green grave of the world.

Of course, her resolve and insight, and even the tentative sense of renewal of a moribund world ("green grave"), come at a cost. Remarking the change from sweetness to sorrow in "Phyllida" (29 October 1927), Travers laments that this "Child of the beauties" is now "marketing loveliness: Grief is on me / For the lips you kiss."

Her last three pieces in the *Irish Statesman* distill the salient themes of her apprenticeship: defining a woman's poetics, celebrating an uninhibited sexuality, and continuing to grow as a consequence of passion and intimacy. "The Poet" (17 December 1927) examines this woman's song as "a still small cry", which makes her sound "like a lost girl / in a wood of fauns." Depending on the reader's perceptions, the next stanza could change the setting from woodland to seashore and the focus from the voice in the head to the thought in the womb, or it could be a generalizing hypothesis derived from the "crying and calling" of the previous stanza.

> There is no woman
> can touch on abundance
> in the teeming world
> of moons and suns
> save in the threaded womb
> that with a silver
> net draws down thought
> to the hidden children.

While both interpretations are tenable and even complementary, the most striking feature of this feminine ontology, for me, is the image of the womb drawing down thought. Travers' metaphor recalls Virginia Woolf's contemporaneous image of a woman writing. In the first draft of her "Professions for Women" speech (21 January 1931), Woolf sees a fisherwoman sitting on the bank of a lake.

> Yes, that is how I see her. She was not thinking; she was not reasoning; she was not constructing a plot; she was letting her imagination down into the depths of her consciousness while she sat above holding on by a thin but quite necessary thread of reason.[9]

Travers' mood is less pensive and more playful in "Prayer in a Field" (25 February 1928). Not merely a plea to the patron saint of lost objects, this "prayer" actually celebrates the lovemaking of the poet and "Michael," which her lost cow used to observe; it also gently berates the celibate for his lack of knowledge, as it tries to shame the saint into returning the cow.

> Have you no girl, Saint Anthony,
> to bend back into Heaven's lawn
> and kiss until your mouth is dry
> for a bowl of milk or spring water?
> If you'd been under a girl's cloak,
> Saint Anthony, now
> you'd know the thirst in Michael's throat
> and bring me home my little cow.

Travers confided to me during our interview that "Prayer in a Field" had been "denounced from the pulpit in Dublin!" In her last poem in the *Irish Statesman*, "Coming Toward Meadows" (17 November 1928), the poet soberly examines where she and her partner find themselves.

> Love, have we come to the end
> Of our wild sojourning?
> Into the passionate wilderness
> Is there no returning?

Although leaving behind "the dark heart of the forest" where they "have hidden" all their "love's thunder," she wonders what lies ahead.

> O whitethorn blowing with red lip
> Fire after fire among the wealds
> Light us a way from the cold brakes
> To the friendly fields!

The brightly colored fruit and stiff-thorned stalks of the *alba spina* hawthorn sum up for Travers the attractions and hazards of sexuality.

While her poetry deals with issues which she has reexamined throughout her career, Travers' early essays in the *Irish Statesman* are more identifiable as first runs for her work in the *New English Weekly*. To her the mingling of the aesthetic and the ordinary, and the sacred and the profane, are subjects appropriate to the artist and the "interpretative" critic as well. In "The Marbles at Carrarra" (12 October 1929), her account of a visit to an Italian mountain town, she muses about the embedding of the strange and the unique within the familiar and the everyday. Upon seeing marble in "all the common necessities of life"—seats, ticket desks, flower beds, wash basins—and realizing that the mode of transport, by pulley and ox cart, has been unchanged for centuries, she dreams of Michelangelo "coming, as year after year he came, wrapped in a dark cloak with shoes of soft flexible leather on his feet, to choose his marbles." Like her head-to-toe picture, Travers' description of the visit flits back and forth in time. On this "golden morning in the Carraras" she feels part of a grand historical continuum, declaring her breakfast of "sour red wine, dry bread and tunny-fish" to be as enjoyable as the Israelites' manna, seeing in every quarryman and sailor "some heroic legendary brigand," and speculating about "the potential Davids and Dawns that lay within the hidden freight of the ships" in the bay. The multiplicity, fullness, and changeability of experience clearly fascinate Travers. Her proto review of a production of Shaw's *The Apple Cart* (26 October 1929) at the Queen's Theatre,

London, begins and ends with references to the multi-faceted and masked nature of this poet-playwright. Although she resorts more to synopsis than she will in later reviews, it is clear that Travers exults in the way Shaw has outraged his Socialist "comrades" with this "apotheosis of kingship" and delights in Shaw's "Mozartian" . . . darting in and out of light and shadow, changing from colour to colour." Her review of "The Italian Pictures" (25 January 1930), a display of painting and sculpture at Burlington House, praises a mingling of outlooks at the same time as it highlights her synaesthetic idiosyncracies. Travers admits being

> tweaked from Heaven to earth and back again, beholding, in a line of three, Botticelli's *Annunciation,* Pollaiolo's *Portrait of a Lady* and Piero della Francesca's *Virgin and Child and Three Angels.* What a pity that nowadays we have lost the art of mixing our worlds so joyously and indiscriminately. With all these saints and haloes, this bright light and brilliant shadow, this accumulation of old passions and griefs, is it any wonder that one forgets the too, too solid whirlpool of flesh about one and feels the stars rising overhead and the immortal meadows breaking into flowers underfoot?

Her ability to enter fully into the world of each painting helps Travers as a critic, and also hints at the beginning of the creative power of her Mary Poppins work. Travers' admiration of Michelangelo's *Holy Boy* as "one of the loveliest marble children in the world . . . with his leonine head breaking out impetuously from the medallion" might have influenced her sketch of Neleus, "The Marble Boy" in *Mary Poppins Opens the Door,* whose "head, with its ruffle of marble curls, was bent towards the water". (92) Even when facing three similarly titled works, Travers explores difference. The *Davids* of Verocchio, Donatello, and Michelangelo appear to her as "three sons of Jesse born under widely differing stars." Verocchio's is a country boy surprised by his "lucky trick" against Goliath; Donatello's is an ambitious lover whose "eyes burn with triumph"; but Michelangelo's is the consummate blend of fighter and singer, with "the strength of his body leashed by his mind's strength." In the Correspondence column of subsequent issues, Travers carries on a spirited but far-from-repentant defense of this review with art critic Thomas Bodkin, who disputes many of her attributions and interpretations. Happy to rank herself "with the vulgar into whose blood the virus of academic criticism that reduces life to terms of comment has not yet entered," she insists on seeing things for herself and on letting "everything . . . shine with its own light" (8 February 1930). Their epistolary joust continues for at least a month, with Bodkin wondering if she is "in full possession of . . . visual and mental faculties" (1 March 1930), and citing Humpty Dumpty as a warning against self-styled hermeneutics. Travers replies that her opponent is like the king's horsemen who "'totted up' the shattered bits of that father of modern thought, Humpty Dumpty," but "could not put him cohesively together again" (8 March 1930). Finally AE, the editor, intervenes and closes the correspondence.

This exchange might have caused Travers to explore in greater detail her own literary, as distinct from philosophic, loyalties and her notion of the critic's role, the topics of the two final essays. "The Other Side of the Penny" (15 February 1930) puts her 'spokesman', the lion, in imaginary debate with "the Philosopher," whose arguments about the dazzling deceits of poetry make him sound like a hybrid of Stephen Gosson and Francis Bacon. Travers counters like a latterday Philip Sidney, that "the poet looks beyond the thing itself, be it form or idea, to the thing's own correspondences and the light it diffuses." Unlike the philosopher, the poet "is enslaved to no system, confined by no boundaries except by that distant skyline that screens the philosopher's Oneness-and-Nothingness." Giddy with this ranging within the zodiac of her own wit and the sight of the retreating philosopher, she lets her 'spokesman' have the last word. "'Praise and blame are the same thing, love and hate touch wings in space, Pure Being is Pure Nothing.'" These apparent antipodes also figure prominently—if not to be reconciled, at least to advance the argument—in "A Brand for the Critic" (12 April 1930). She dismisses all critical work as a "multitude of literary cheepings," contributing to the subspecies of "'twitterature,'" and pins up her personal (yet conventionally Arnoldian) colors: "True criticism is, surely, a process of inclusion, not of separation, of preoccupation with the thing for the thing's own sake and not a pronouncement of the critic's preconceived ideas about that thing." Travers demands more than "mere carping" or "pedantic commentary on dates, names, cracks and precedent," but esteems "the interpretative critic who looks at a picture with more than eyes, hears music with more than ears, whose aim is not to break art up into a thousand fragments but to see it whole." Such a paragon, she maintains, is truly a creative artist, deeply affected by "that triple stream" of "intuition, reason and imagination."

This stream influences her own work in the *New English Weekly,* of which I will only discuss the poetry here. Two poems about childhood, or perceptions of the child, frame the other pieces concerning sexuality and womanhood set against what can only be called a cosmic stage. The childhood poems are inherently religious. "Noel" (21 December 1933) has the simple directness of a carol, with its two quartets telescoping the central Christian events of Incarnation and Crucifixion.

> Child in the manager laid
> > Take now your myrrh and gold
> And incense as we kneel
> > With the three kings of old.
>
> Child of the gentle heart
> > Do you know that we mean
> To crucify you
> > When the leaves are green?

The original version actually opened with an invocation to the "Child of the bright head," and the main verb in the second stanza was "guess" rather than "mean." Travers informed me of these "improvements" during our interview; the changes focus attention on the paradoxes of the Christ Child and the acceptance of sacrifice by the guiltless one. The last poem grapples with the mysteries of Christmas and Easter as perceived by children. "A Memory of Childhood" (23 December 1937) recreates a Christmas celebration from Travers' Australian past. Set "in the sugar fields so green-o," the opening scene is festive and carefree, with its string of hyphenated and elongated words suggesting the gay, tambourine-punctuated rhythms of a linked dance.

> The father wore a silken coat
>   With an ear-ring in his ear-o,
> And silk of crimson about his throat
> And a wide-brimmed, straw-brimmed, grass-trimmed hat
>   Like a Spanish bandolero.

The arrival of the "strange man bruising the sugar-cane," whom the children do not know to be the draper's man delivering their mother's new gown, abruptly shifts the tone from gaiety to awful reverence. (Perhaps in using this phrase, Travers herself, as one of "the three little children" and a student of the piano, was recalling the Schumann impressionistic tone picture [Opus 68, number 29] titled "The Strange Man" [*Fremder Mann* from *Album für die Jungen*].) Identifying their stranger as "the King of Heaven," the children kneel. Travers captures this obeisance in a final stanza that, in emulating the earlier carefree tone, and with a significant lowering of the last syllable, serves as a meditative coda.

> They knelt to the lord, the holy child,
>   That was in Bethlehem-o,
> And climbed the heavy hill and died
> With a wicked robber on either side
>   And died for each of them.
>   Oh!

Closing prayers do not characterize Travers' other submissions. The most lighthearted, however, "Zodiac Circus" (11 January 1934), ends with the sleeping of the planets, which have been whipped by the circus-master Sun around the ring, and the coming of the day. The poem has the interplanetary, grandiose frenzy of the Grand Chain, the Celestial Circus, and the High-Tide Party from the Mary Poppins books. Saturn the clown somersaults, Venus the ballerina leaps through a hoop, Jupiter the muscle man pumps iron, Mars swallows swords, Neptune directs a troupe of seals, while Earth and Uranus juggle and sing. And finally, Pluto is a black minstrel, and Mercury a trapezist. The details of Earth and Uranus kissing in the wings and the poet's wanting Mercury, who is also a gambler, to bend her "back against the dark blue tent / After the show" do not, of course, have any parallels in the Mary Poppins festivities. For, although the poems indulge in dreams of harmony and reconciliation, the realization of these states is very much in the future. "In Time of Trouble" (25 January 1934) concentrates on the phoenix, "burning bird," and the salamander, "the spotted flame-fed child," as the only figures who do not burn in the fire. The poet, by contrast, is associated with the refrain, "Oh, I am sick and I must die / and burn up in my own desire." She does, however, foresee a time when the universe loves, harmony overcomes discord, and the salamander mates with the phoenix. The resultant apocalyptic, pentecostal period looks back to the prophets and ahead to the seconds "inside the crack," which she later describes in *Happy Ever After* (1940):

> Night with day, leopard with kid
> shall then lie down and man's dark sun
> and the bright darknesses of woman
> fuse and divide and be again
> whole light, whole darkness and upon
> the falling continents and coasts
> love shall lie down with lust and breed
> a million holy ghosts;
> and the dreams of the old
> and the visions of the young
> shall alight together
> upon one fiery tongue.

"Water and Stone" (15 February 1934) depicts female and male as "the river's daughter" and the "man of stone," respectively. Their coupling is a confrontation of "great foemen in one bed," which involves an altering of normal characteristics.

> Naked he within her stream
> And naked she encircling him
> Must battle give and may not cease
> Till rock have motion, water peace.

The female figure in "The Dark Heart" (26 March 1936) seems initially to be unalterable: "Stiller than stone / Immutable and bowed." The darkness of the heart "That has for its business / The root and the seed" could be her sterility, against which the narrator–observer suggests various disguises from the surrounding vegetation and animal life.

> Press through the heifer's flank
> Where her cheek bends,
> Run in the jets of milk
> Down through her hands
>
> And when the evening tides
> Brim up and to her stream
> Her naked lover goes,
> Lord, go thou in with him!

The remaining two poems, "Sun in Cancer" (1 March 1934), and "Song in Season" (31 March 1934), are less oppositional and dyadic. Although the speaker warns the "Sun" to move warily "in the House of the Crab," the feminine, encompassing power of the zodiac sign is clearly the issue, a power presented positively in sexually charged metaphors.

> So that at last her darkness may transcend
> she sleeps not, waiting, steady as a star

to draw into her harbourage
that fiery mariner

And headlong downward thrust his hissing spark—
that ever-cooling plummet plunging there
fathoms her utmost lightless deep
then falls and makes no stir.

In contrast to the friction and plangency most of her poems dramatize, "Song in Season" is jocular and ebullient, and seductively so. Her lover, a persuasive logician, extolls her breasts as "sweeter than cherry cake," and adds "and I *love* cherry cake." What distinguishes this dialogue from her more turbulent pieces is its attempt to emulate the candor of the first and last poems.

Then said he "Oh, love should be
Bright as candles on Christmas trees,
Simple and sweet and rational,
No clash of dreams or heavy fall
Of heart against the white and red
Confines of this lovely breast,
No cloudy thought trouble the mind
That has informed this mouth, this thigh
With delicate serenity.
O bird under the burdened tree
Love should come gaily as the may
Flowers up. I think it is no sin
To laugh and laughing take love in.
So doing we shall slip the chain
That holds love captive in the brain
And catch him fresh before he's grown
Hoary with thought and overblown
With longing—*that's* the miracle!"
"Well?" said he.
　　　　　　And I said "Well."

The Christmas poems were not, however, without allusion to the unravelled consequences of the Nativity in the Crucifixion. Although the lover announces his position unequivocally and laughingly, his beloved's monosyllabic reaction and the tortuous debating of most of Travers' other poems argue against this blitheness. Despite the implied wish that matters were otherwise, such a poem underscores the painful connections between desire and dilemma.

Blending reason and emotion, acuity and playfulness, Travers' early poems and essays offer more than a record of a maturing artistic sensibility. They lay the groundwork for her exploration of a mythic, essentially mysterious universe and search for the reconciliation of opposites, themes Travers later pursued in her theater criticism and, with even greater subtlety, in the Poppins canon itself.

3

Reviewing in the
New English Weekly:
Seeing the Object as It Really Is

> The Theatre . . . is the authentic link between per-
> son and person, the common denominator of human-
> ity and the means by which the dramatic element in
> man is released and projected into actuality. We
> know ourselves not merely by inward but also by
> outward looking and the theatre, of all the second-
> ary arts, provides the greatest natural arena for the
> clash or contact of self with other.
>
> *New English Weekly,* 13 May 1937

The masthead of the *New English Weekly* (1932–49) announced
that it was "a review of public affairs, literature and the arts."
During her sixteen-year association with this periodical, from
1933 to its demise, Travers served primarily as drama critic with
additional contributions as book and film reviewer, travel essayist, foreign correspondent, and poet. She was a member of the
Editorial Advisory Committee along with T. S. Eliot, and actually
reviewed early performances of his *Murder in the Cathedral* and
The Family Reunion as well as his *Old Possum's Book of Practical
Cats.* She assessed productions of Shakespeare at the Old Vic,
Stratford, and many theatres in between, feeling no qualms at
drubbing performances by John Gielgud, Charles Laughton,
Laurence Olivier, and Paul Scofield. Her critic's pen was never
acerbic or pedantic, but usually witty and engaging. After reading

her almost weekly essays, I am impressed by the sheer volume of her work during a period when the first three Mary Poppins books appeared, a book of traveler's letters describing her experiences in Russia was issued (from copy for the *New English Weekly*), her *I Go by Sea, I Go by Land* was published, and four privately printed Christmas and New Year's gift books were circulated to friends. Equally impressive are the consistent high quality, self-possessed voice, and critical acumen of her writing. There are no traces of hesitancy or gawkishness and no periods of the ferocity or unreachable standards which often mark the beginner. Rather than indicating the growth of an artistic consciousness, Travers' criticism shows its expansiveness and assurance. Whether ascribed to P.T., Pamela Travers, or the almost anagrammatic "Milo Reve," her reviews are identifiable by a series of common themes. Among these are the need to join ideas and people, to engage an audience or readership with fully realized and fallible humanity, to overact and exult in gallimaufry, to provide entertainment which is faithful to reality and to avoid cleverness and mawkishness at all costs. She undertakes reviewing in the Arnoldian sense of seeing the object as it really is. Of course these esteemed principles do not preclude severe statements about fallings-off; as a matter of fact the sound, heartfelt nature of Travers' opinions about the theater, and art in general, leads her to criticize as forcefully as she does. She inveighs against the "antimacassar of gentility" in which the theater is wrapped, laments with a funeral dirge, the fact that Snow White, the "celluloid heroine," was the outstanding theatrical event of 1938, discounts academic "attitudinizing" as empty and futile, and searches desperately for new playwrights as the London stage "scrapes the bottom of the barrel." In all her reviews she shows the depth of her commitment to the first principles of theater and of art. The personal authorial voice is strong in Travers' criticism, which is dotted with anecdotes and childhood reminiscences. The distinguishing feature of her criticism is that she measures each particular performance against her own carefully articulated concept of the individual work and its complexities.

Her early publication, *Moscow Excursion* (1934), not only shows Travers' astuteness as a traveler, but also sheds light on the adventurous, unencumbered, ingenuous young woman she was. Aware of the stir her travel plans have caused among her circle of acquaintances, (who see her decision as "either the Chance of a Lifetime or a Piece of Utter Recklessness,") she presents herself to the reader—in a sketch that might impress postmodernists, for whom all action is political, as disingenuous—as an apolitical observer, one for whom "it is difficult . . . to think or feel politically."[1] This unaligned observer is quickly caught up, however, in shipboard debates involving "groups of fanatically vocal cells crystallising and disintegrating, . . . a sort of grand chain of conversation (or argument) where one never holds the same hand for more than a moment" (8). As part of an enthusiastic but motley assortment of tourists, monitored and lectured to by hectoring guides, Travers soon tires of the diet of statistics. Her increasing weariness in this "mechanised rather than . . . humanised state" (xi) is evident in her descriptions: the Smolny Institute is the "Russian variant" (22) of Bethlehem and St. Isaac's Cathedral, with faith turned "in another direction, . . . is now an anti-God museum" (26–27). Travers longs for delicacies like lettuce, and ordinary amenities like plugs in the bathtub (as opposed to her makeshift corks). Terming Russia "this *prison!*," deeming it "a vast negation" (52), she misses genuine human communication, what she calls "the *person* in the eyes" (44). Her only truly enjoyable times significantly, are at the theater, where she sees *Hamlet,* and at the ballet, where she encounters "the perfect audience", and feels "that rare sense of harmony that comes when a great number of people are equally sharing in delight" (98).

One of Travers' first loves is Shakespeare, and so it seems wise to start any analysis of her reviews with an examination of her essays on seventeen Shakespearean plays—roughly half of the canon. Occasionally she wrote about a single play, *Hamlet,* for instance, as many as five times. At the opening of a very favorable review of Alec Guiness's production of *Twelfth Night,* Travers pauses to relate some of her reflections "in off-Drama moments" about William Shakespeare as both an abstract and a human composite:

> He is one with the impersonal nouns—love, wisdom, science, pain, Shakespeare. Then I look at a programme and am drawn back to the concrete, the embodied word; to the hand that actually wrote "Shakespeare" and which turns out to belong to William—to Will, even—a common-or-garden compact of blood and lymph and bone that one might bump up against any day walking around in time. I like him this way, too. . . . William worked in time but his design, his Shakespeareness—if I may coin the word—was in eternity. (30 September 1948)

The dual nature of the timeless artist and the approachable contemporary informs all of Travers' Shakespeare criticism.

Two plays on which she expends a lot of superlatives and philosophizes about light, shadow, and gift are *The Tempest* and *A Midsummer Night's Dream*. The quality of any production of *The Tempest* can be judged, according to Travers, by the performance of "the trio of Prospero-earth, Ariel-air and Caliban-waters-under-earth" (15 February 1934). The play's "eternal elements" consist of Prospero "climbing the arrogant heights of mind," yet providing "a dying fall, an air of fading dream"; Ariel, "compact of light, love's shadow still unknown"; and Caliban, "the dark mind, still to be lit by love," yet retaining "a sort of childlike sadness" (23 July 1936). For each deficiency in the Old Vic Performance of 1934 Travers prescribes an antidote. She resuscitates and valorizes ranting by pointing out, for Charles Laughton's benefit, that "nothing but *more* ranting, more swashbuckling and less good taste, will approximate present-day acting to the quality necessary for Shakespeare" (15 February 1934). (By the way, Travers' repeated claims about the ranting and overacting she thinks so characteristic of the Elizabethan playhouse have been disproved. Excavations in February and March 1989, uncovering the Rose Theatre, indicate an intimate space, most suited to refined, minimal gesturing.) She reminds Elsa Lanchester that

Ariel is a native of the upper air and not a Mabel Lucie Atwell fairy. The "clear bucolic gaiety" she senses in one of several out-door performances buttresses her claim that *The Tempest,* "far more than any propaganda play, argue(s) best against war" (14 July 1938).

Two performances of *A Midsummer Night's Dream,* in Regent's Park (8 July 1937) and in the courtyard of an old inn in South-wark (12 May 1949), prompt her descant on similar themes of light, darkness, and gift; predictably, mixtures more inclined to brightness and innocence predominate. Venting her long-stand-ing animus toward Barrie's character, Peter Pan, she insists that the play should not be turned "into a highbrow appendix to Peter Pan" (8 July 1937), and that to preserve the essence of this magic it should remain "penny plain."

Despite their celebration of light and beauty, Travers' reviews are never far removed from the specter and effects of war, influ-ences which are most prominent in her essays on productions of *Julius Caesar, Coriolanus, Richard II,* and *Richard III.* She praises the modern-dress, Embassy production of *Julius Caesar,* wedging it tightly into the outlook of 1939. "Now . . . when dicta-tors are four a penny and we ourselves no more in anybody's sight than the poorest creature in the Roman mob, this three-hundred-year-old piece of politico-poetical fustian is more topical and up-to-date than the daily journals and the news from the B.B.C." (21 December 1939). Whether in togas or bowlers, the characters are clearly recognizable in terms of their contemporary counterparts. "Caesar, intoxicated with the fumes of his own splendour, is a composite portrait of Hitler, Franco and Mussolini; Marc Antony may be heard any day on the radio propaganda or on Sunday is to be seen in Hyde Park. As for Brutus—do we not stand submis-sive in the pubs while he tells us, by permission of the B.B.C., the latest doings of our own House of Commons?"

Travers is always acutely aware of the poetry of Shakespearean politics. Coriolanus's "terrible integrity" stamps him as "Shake-speare's one true soldier, blind in the hither eye as all soldiers must be and fundamentally innocent and childlike as every sol-dier is" (12 May 1938). Almost a decade later, when the experiences of soldiers and war were being analyzed and sifted, she corroborates and extends her earlier view of Coriolanus as being pigheaded, with the assertion that he has "that curious flowerlike look of the professional soldier" (22 April 1948). Travers examines political machinations from the aspects of the game and poetry involved. Without mounting a hero or dethroning a villain, she considers the "double-threaded fate" of Richard II, "the man of action rising on the tide, the emotional man ebbing with its fall" (21 October 1937). Later she sympathizes with this "King of Sorrows" who, "out of his enforced lowliness . . . creates, with meglomaniac perseverance, an inverted grandeur full of messianic overtones that make Bolingbroke, for all his usurped crown, look pale and puny beside him" (12 June 1947). Richard III, by contrast, is "the king of villains, black to the bone, a brand upon the memory" (17 February 1949). The problem, as Travers sees it, with Laurence Olivier's Richard is that he is a diminished whitewash, "not nearly physically repellent enough: not Richard Crookback but a nice mixture of Jane Eyre's Mr. Rochester and a pantomime Demon King!"

When she comes to review the tragedies of Lear, Antony and Cleopatra, Othello, Macbeth, and Hamlet, the problems of motive and design are more unsettling than either the duality of Richard II, or the unalloyed heinousness of Richard III. Her descriptions of these plays are not mere lecture notes, nor rough drafts for *Scrutiny* or the *Shakespeare Quarterly*. They are reviews, lush with images and indulging in bursts of abandon and sweeping statements. If they are criticism at all, they are offshoots of G. Wilson Knight's roughly contemporaneous examination of the poetic elements and celebration of the visionary wholeness and mystification of each play, *The Wheel of Fire* (1930) and *The Imperial Theme* (1931). *King Lear* is for Travers "a soul's history, . . . the light of consciousness breaking upon the dark of selfhood" (7 May 1936). Travers' penchant for universalizing stamps many of these reviews. When considering *Othello,* which she terms "a tricksy play, [with] none of its major characters . . . clearly defined" (17 February 1938), she is very decisive about the interpretations of the key roles. In the title role Ralph Richardson impressed her as "a perfect, if oddly coloured, English Gentleman, reeking of buttercup fields and the Home Counties," instead of "a great guileless nature driven beyond its confines by a baser nature's cunning," which he should have been. A similar divide between actualization and concept separates Michael Redgrave's Macbeth from her understanding of what the role should be. Redgrave played "the gangster chieftain of a boy's comic, elocuting without reason," while Travers wanted to see "the man of desperate imagination swept like a leaf before his daemon will" (5 February 1948). Although she considers Macbeth "even more metaphysical than Hamlet" (5 February 1948), it is *Hamlet* that supplies her with the true measure of a tragic performance. There are, of course, predictable numbers of colossal failures. Among these are John Gielgud's rarefied Hamlet, which made Travers feel "each actor was kept alive only by repeated sips from a posset made by soaking a First Folio in tepid water" (10 June 1937); Leslie Howard's overmild "lullaby Hamlet for the cradles of Manhattan" (10 June 1937); Wolfit's weepy, unintellectual Hamlet (4 November 1937) or his Hamlet in aspic, "the gloomy Dean rather than the gloomy Dane" (4 April 1946); and Guiness's mild, insufficiently neurotic version of the "impoverished undergraduate turned undertaker" (24 November 1938). Travers insists that *Hamlet* be overacted and promises that it will triumph over the meanest surroundings. As illustration she offers this charming childhood memory:

> I remember seeing "Hamlet" played in the school hall of a mining town in Australia. The show began at ten instead of the scheduled eight o'clock because the company, travelling by lorry from town to town, did not notice that the Hamlet of the evening had inadvertently fallen off as they rounded a bend. He had walked the last ten miles carrying the suitcase he had been clutching at the time of the accident, and, spurred by unkind fate and the furious catcalls of the waiting audience, he and the rest of the company gave the best performance of "Hamlet" I have ever seen. The echo still resounds. It is just this element, this instant burst of clamour that the Wimbledon production lacks. (4 November 1937)

Despite the expertise in sets, lighting, and costumes in Olivier's filmed *Hamlet,* she finds this very sophisticated export impossible to believe, externalized, and oversimplified (3 June 1948). In general, Travers is unimpressed because, as she argues in her review of Leslie Howard's *Romeo and Juliet,* films are mere "incidentals" in contrast to Shakespeare's "essence" (10 June 1937).

Her comments on the comedies tend to be fewer and distinguished mainly by some very strong dislikes. *The Merchant of Venice,* for instance, "glances off emotions without truly contacting them" (19 May 1938), and *The Taming of the Shrew* is a "tedious," insensitive, not even very funny "jape" (15 April 1937; 20 November 1947). When played with the speed of light and the right combination of "bubble-blown laughter" and day-dream moods, without stress on hoydenism and skittishness, *Twelfth Night* (24 September 1936; 30 September 1948), *Much Ado* (22 June 1939), and *As You Like It* (4 July 1946) are, however, radiant "galliards and corantos" of comedy.

Her reviews, ranging from works by Shakespeare's contemporaries and predecessors to his successors, show Travers' love of all theatrical forms and acute ear for language. She believes that the theatre is indivisible and whole, "the sophisticated and commercial drama [being] at the other end of the stick from the morality play" (25 July 1946). So completely does Travers enter the milieu of each performance that, on occasion, she offers the directors suggestions for doing things more appropriately or whimsically. Noting that Medwall's Tudor interlude, *Fulgens and Lucrece,* was written for an "archiepiscopal banquet," she advises that in the place of "pale-faced and tweedy-kneed" members of the audience on stage, "a row of painted, cardboard bishops might conceivably have given it the necessary air of unreality and leant it wings" (2 April 1936). At times, though, her assessments of a playwright's complete work, based only on a single performance, are simply too sweeping. Not only does she persist in calling John Webster (whose two tragedies were probably written around 1612) an Elizabethan dramatist, but she also launches a wholesale condemnation of the artist—"Webster cannot deal with goodness or sorrow; he lacks the fibre for them" (24 April 1947)—after seeing one presentation of *The White Devil*. Webster's Duchess of Malfi and Bosola are palpable examples to disprove her claim. She is equally tough with Christopher Marlowe. After seeing a revival of *Doctor Faustus* she reasons that Marlowe's "false mountains of rhetoric" make him "out of tune with our modern mind" (11 November 1948). Perhaps the space of forty years accounts for the difference between Travers' view and our own—although Harry Levin's landmark study *The Overreacher* (1952) was in the offing. In fact, since Marlowe's mastery of rhetoric and levels of embedded allusion are the subjects of lively academic debate, Travers' censorious judgement seems, itself, to be out of tune.

If we examine her reviews in terms of the chronology of the plays involved, we find her criticism just as assured and severe when she moves from the Restoration, with a sympathetic glance at Congreve's Lady Wishfort (11 November 1948), to the nineteenth and twentieth centuries, surveying Ibsen, Chekhov, and Shaw as well as her own contemporaries.

Distinct from the multiplicity of Ibsen are the singularity and predominant mordancy of Chekhov, whose characters brood "on the meaning of life and death" (30 December 1948). Her Chekhov criticism, on *The Seagull, Three Sisters,* and *The Cherry Orchard,* strives to accord appropriate but not excessive respect to an artist, whom she considers "a petit maître" (18 June 1936). Praise is kept within certain sensible bounds. Finding the influence of samovars and vodka too oppressive in an English adaptation of Bulgakov, Travers quips about the generally "stony ground" of Russian drama: "The theatrical prospect of three sisters *forever* chasing a seagull in a cherry orchard is almost too much for one critic to endure" (20 October 1938).

In reviewing six Ibsen plays, Travers neatly distills the essence of each, while she conveys an admiration for the inexorable, inevitable mechanism "like a packed spool unwinding slowly and solemnly" (17 June 1948). The one exception is *Peer Gynt,* which she terms an uncertain "nineteenth-century jumble of satire, dream and allegory" (21 May 1936). Although she questions the change of title to *Nora,* Travers nevertheless captures the central idea of *A Doll's House:* "the waste inherent in a life of intimacy that at no point touches reciprocal love" (16 February 1939). Her observations on *The Wild Duck* (25 November 1948) are the most poignant. She mistakenly calls it a "pause of pure feeling" between *A Doll's House* and *Ghosts* (the correct timeframes would be *Ghosts* [1881] and *Hedda Gabler* [1890]). Quibbling about dates does not, however, lessen the truth of her contention that each character "is a wild duck, far from home, seeking by means of illusion some support for his insupportable loneliness." She finds such "poetry, pathos and human sensibility" in the play that it becomes—in what sounds like an aside from Mary Poppins, particularly the "Full Moon" chapter of *Mary Poppins* (1934)—"a Grand Chain of inner Ibsens, each aspect taking another by the hand in a tremendous effort at reconciliation."

For Travers, there is nothing formulaic or necessarily inevitable about Shaw. He is, she declares, "our most modern, perhaps indeed our only modern dramatist," who even at his most "frivolous and fairy-taleish," as in *You Never Can Tell,* remains "limber and sinewy" (30 October 1947). Of course her praise of Shaw—as the scourge of the Edwardians, who became "the canonized hero of the middlebrows"; as the "plumber to the theatre", who spring-cleaned its parlours and drainpipes; and as the artist who renounced poetry to become the "play-boy among the philosophers" (7 October 1937)—does not preclude stern indictments of his failures. *Cymbeline* is an unnecessary and a pedestrian whittling-down of the original (2 December 1937); *Geneva,* with its characterization of Hitler, Mussolini, and Franco as elderly Fabians, does not provide even a crumb of wisdom for a troubled time (15 December 1938); and *In Good King Charles' Golden Days* is an irrelevant trifle, at a time when guns rumble and the furniture shakes during a London air raid (30 May 1940). Her most favorable reviews focus on the compassion and degree of humanity displayed in performances of *Candida* (8 May 1947) and *Saint Joan* (29 January 1948).

Very few of Travers' contemporaries approach, in her opinion, the standards of Ibsen, Chekhov, and Shaw, especially in terms of linking emotions and ideas, and placing both in real people. She decries the transformation of characters into mere ciphers or mouthpieces, bereft of ordinary humanity and therefore isolated from our compassion, and on that account criticizes Eugene O'Neill, Noel Coward, Emlyn Williams, Somerset Maugham, Terence Rattigan, and even J. B. Priestley. As Travers sees it, O'Neill's *Anna Christie* resorts to a "platitudinous moral and sentimental compromise" (6 May 1937); *Mourning Becomes Electra* is a "merry-go-round of human passions," providing a cut-rate "subscription to a library of psychological works" that prove "all God's chillun got complexes nowadays" (20 January 1938); and *Desire under the Elms* (8 February 1940) is a crudely staged burlesque. Travers reviews six Priestley plays in all; although she finds them full and, to a degree, entertaining, his characters remain for her types, "coat-hangers holding up the latest fashion in literary humanity" (30 November 1939), and "not sufficiently alive-alive-o" (2 October 1947).

Her hopes of transfusing new blood into the theater, or of its being galvanized by a new dramatic voice, in the joint works of W. H. Auden and Christopher Isherwood, or in Christopher Fry's plays fade fast, while A. A. Milne soon loses all credibility for Travers. The Anglicized caricature of Hitler and the fictional kingdoms of Westland and Ostnia, in the Auden–Isherwood collaboration, *On the Frontier* (23 February 1939), impress Travers as too familiar and transparent, and the playwrights' dilatory caution causes her to lament that it is too soon for them to wear their trousers rolled. What she sees as their mother fixation, in *The Ascent of F6,* explains her caustic comments about these "poets in a play-pen" mouthing the message of "childish defeatism", which was "piped into being by Peter Pan" (20 July 1939). She sees little reason to resuscitate or encourage Milne's "drama of Whimsey-Whamsey" (27 May 1937), which she judges "as satisfying as skim milk" (8 December 1938).

She adduces various reasons for dissatisfaction—from the unnecessary to the incomplete aspects of the works involved. For Travers the dramatizations of novels by Bronte (22 April 1937), Steinbeck (8 June 1939), and James (7 May 1946) miss the point in much the same way as film versions of Shakespeare. When she reviews the presentation of religious topics in drama, Travers demands a critical honesty of the playwrights which she rarely finds. The sanitized Saint Paul, in *Chastity, My Brother* by Ben Travers (not a relation), gives no hint of "the rising, swelling, transforming yeast of sensuality" (28 May 1936). Travers holds out most hope for the plays of Dorothy Sayers. Reviewing a strong performance of *The Zeal of Thy House* at the Westminster Theatre, she argues for mounting religious drama in a church, where it would be "more effectively at home in transept and nave." As she reasons, "only in that atmosphere, in which the very stones are permeated by a great idea, can a religious performance create the necessary echo" (14 April 1938). The production of *The Devil to Pay,* Sayers' reworking of the Faust legend, at the Canterbury Festival, saddens Travers, however, because the vast potential of a modern Faustus has not been realized. After the performance, as Travers and the vesturer hunt through the dark cathedral in search of a program, she reflects for a moment, in a fashion reminiscent of Arnold's thoughts on the "Sea of Faith" in "Dover Beach." "In the empty chapels our footsteps rang with the sound of a thousand feet. Night that brings all things home had peopled the arched caverns with invisible throngs from the centuries and it seemed for a moment as if the great shell echoed once more with the sound of its old sea" (29 June 1939).

The single instance of consistent praise in her reviews of works by contemporaries involves the poet-playwright, T. S. Eliot. Her reviews of *The Family Reunion* and *Murder in the Cathedral* laud Eliot's handling of the historical past in light of the present. Accordingly, she bases endorsement of *The Family Reunion* on Eliot's use of the moment "as a sieve through which the past is poured on its way to become the future" (6 April 1939). Her assessment of *Murder in the Cathedral* is considerably less glib and more direct in celebrating the text itself. Although she does not cover its first performance in the Chapter House in Canterbury, the Old Vic production convinces her of Eliot's success in collecting Becket's whitened, scattered bones and stretching upon them "not merely the semblance of a prelate centuries dead but the very skin of modern man" (1 July 1937). Not often so laudatory, Travers' critical voice can be ironic, with an edge that approaches satire. On occasion she adopts the persona of a letter writer called "Cora" who, after accompanying "Ethel" to a performance, decides to drop a line to their mutual friend "Mabel", conveying her impressions of an "ever-so-nice" outing. Aside from the deliberate grammatical howlers, the missives allow Travers to indulge in a certain mock ingenuousness that proves devastating. About St. John Irvine's *People of Our Class* Cora writes, "You don't have to think about anything and at the same time its awfully deep and makes you realize and that's the sort of play that appeals to Ethel and I" (16 June 1938). A similar breathlessness informs her report of O'Neill's *Desire under the Elms,* which the censor has just released, as Cora reasons, "because the war is on I suppose and people probably won't notice so much because with a dreadful thing like a war on everything else seems much less dreadful" (8 February 1940). Cora tries valiantly to explain the play's love of the soil—even though "after all you can see a bit of that pretty nearly anywhere at any time"—as well as the old gentleman's "bad temper": "As Ethel said, you would be too if you were an old man of seventy-six and had gone to all that trouble to have a baby and then to discover it wasn't your baby but your son's baby and on top of that to have your third wife smother the baby in its little wooden cradle. You see Mabel it is all very, very earthy." The antagonist throughout these letters is the frowning, bespectacled, severe, male drama critic, next to whom the hapless duo are invariably seated. When this bearded fellow, who they are convinced is "a Nazi spy," berates Eugene O'Neill, Cora protests, "We didn't know why he had to bring Eugene O'Neill up in a play by the censor but he went on and on and said Mr. O'Neill was out to bruise people's minds rather than enlighten them and that he must have gotten his ideas of primitive life out of a Middle West novel because they were so conventional and literary that no actor could hope to give them human shape." "P. T.", herself, promotes the fiction of being a male reviewer, calling for a race of "mighty, majestic mean old men" (16 December 1937) to undertake the critic's role, referring to a time when "we . . . were boys together" (7 April 1938), and labeling the critic (who, in this "diatribe" against the Old Vic, deserves free tickets) as "the man of judgment" temporarily forced underground as "the man of the maquis" (17 October 1946). It would be facile to assume that this accomplished woman needed the weight of maleness to support or shore up her criticism. Travers confounds contemporary theorizing about the self-conscious female authorial voice; she seems, instead, to take a farceur's delight in sending up conventional notions of male authorship by deploying them so well.

The scanty observations she does make about specific female roles show that Travers sees women as intuitively, albeit nonverbally aware of their equal and complementary rights. "When was any Shakespeare woman unaware?" (24 September 1936) she quips in a review of a *Twelfth Night* performance. This assessment of acuteness informs her views not only of Viola but of Beatrice, Kate, Rosalind, Juliet, Volumnia, Cordelia, Desdemona, and Cleopatra. Such asseverations sound romantic and quaint today, when feminist criticism has produced so many different and unsettling examinations of the silences of women in Shakespeare; when both women (for example Kathleen McLuskie) and men (Peter Erickson) are labeling Shakespeare patriarchal; when critics such as Elaine Showalter are cogently announcing the need to tell anew the story of Ophelia; and when readers such as Madelon Sprengnether are questioning the capacity of Coriolanus for intimacy, in light of his mother's influence.[2]

Travers' comments on non-Shakespearean women impress me as a mixture of clear-sighted career-woman's judgements and pure mush. In reviewing Claire Boothe's *The Women,* she perceptively judges that, in the society of the play, the discord between "those two chimeras," status and acquisitions, preoccupies and consequently silences individual women, who are propitiated "as the Pythoness in the temple" (11 May 1939). Travers' advice to Catherine Sloper, jilted by the fortune hunter Morris Townsend, in *The Heiress* (based on Henry James's *Washington Square*), shows that she considers women capable of forgiveness and nurturance as well as direction and control. She suggests that if Miss Sloper is as mature, "strong-minded," and discerning as we are asked to believe, then she should actually open the door to her "betrayer" when he returns, rather than locking it. Travers goes as far as to suggest a marriage, with Catherine, however, exerting a smug control. "She could have devised some means of keeping her hand upon the purse-strings, she could have had her longed-for pink and blue family, she might even conceivably—and how she could have tortured him in the process!—have turned him into a human being, even to the extent of making him love her" (3 March 1949). There is a sour taste, a dishearteningly manipulative subtext in the projected "conventional" ending.

A similar combination of trenchant opinion and rare bursts of benignity is evident in her periodic reviews of works for children. Travers never pooh poohs the importance or reverberations of childhood events. St. John Hawkins' *Return of the Prodigal* triggers fond recollections of her family's beachcomber friend, a possible model for Robertson Ay, the Banks's man-of-no-work. Travers' own "ne'er-do-well" hero collected strange shells from the Great Barrier Reef and in "between gargantuan bouts of drunkenness wrote verses shell-like in elegance and intricacy" (3 February 1949). Travers judges both the regressive childishness of Peter Pan, to whom she was probably introduced as a child, and the cloying sweetness of Christopher Robin, whom she encountered as an adult, impossible to "thole" (27 May 1937). She resorts to no such Irishisms when she takes aim at the two Disney cartoons for 1938, "Mickey Mouse" and "Snow White," objecting to the anthropomorphic tendencies of the former, and denouncing the unctuous sanctimony of the latter. She admonishes the creators of "Mickey Mouse" that in place of the animation of "semi-human emotions" the audience deserves a fairy tale spectacle that builds on "moment-to-moment absurdity" (3 February 1938). Because children are "natural moralists," she reminds them, the *truly* melodramatic character in "Snow White" remains the midnight hag. At the heart of Disney's "enlargement of the animal world," Travers discovers "a corresponding deflation of all human values" and "a profound cynicism at the root" (21 April 1938). For exactly opposite reasons, she lavishes praise on Eliot's *Old Possum's Book of Practical Cats* and Beatrix Potter's tales. She delights in the fiction that Eliot's ditties, masterpieces of erudition, are the results of "arduous research" in feline ways (14 December

1939), and applauds Potter's brief, chastened style, its "underlying irony and non-nonsense quality that does not shrink from terrible happenings" (10 April 1947). In her review of Margaret Lane's biography of Potter, Travers, writing as "Milo Reve", posits some definitive principles governing the writing of stories for children: the book must please the author, must be told to the "hidden child" within the author, and, in its combination of "ignorance and innocence," must be a "primer of magic and wisdom." It is curious that, although talking about a female writer and having herself, at this point, three Mary Poppins books to her credit, she still refers, as in her theater criticism, to the author as masculine (see the appendix).

For Travers, very few books indeed meet these high principles. When such old favorites as *Little Women* and Mary Lamb's *Mrs. Leicester's School*, along with new books like *The Mad O'Haras* and *The Young Traveller in Australia*, come across her desk for review, Travers embraces them with an enthusiastic hug and gives an occasional glimpse of her own childhood. She appreciates Alcott's "feeling for values and . . . underlying conviction that children have hearts to be used as well as sensations to be stimulated," and grants that Mary Lamb, with her tender, amusing stories and telescopic eye for detail, "understood children all through" (2 December 1948). She admits having been "a bit of a Mad O'Hara" in her day, and especially enjoys the travelogue because of the genteel memories it evokes. "When I was a child the only way I could learn about other countries was by reading missionary tracts given me by my pious piano-teacher, so that today almost every quarter of the globe has for me a faint flavour of old hymn-books." Her case for the Grimm Brothers is an impassioned plea to know the fairy tales, "which means really living them as experience." Just as there is no need to sanitize or bowdlerize the tales for children, who are "all Old Testament characters with strong stomachs and a bias towards elementary justice," there should be no credence given to the "delusion" that fairy tales are simply "diversions." "Since their primary concern is with good and evil, the nature of the world and the possibility of change, none of us is too old to be involved" (9 December 1948). But, sadly, one aspect of childhood that remains closed to adults is the purity of children's play, which she calls being "all alone in now" (9 June 1949).

One of the many remarkable features of Travers' occasional essays is her ability to immerse herself in the present, and yet see it against a cosmic, mythical backdrop. Whether discussing events as mundane as dog and motor shows, or as unusual as picnicking in winter or forgetting her customary tube station, these essays are always speculative explorations of patterns that are larger than the single event or moment. Often they are also links to, or forecasts of, episodes in the Mary Poppins books. Reporting on such a prosaic occasion as a dog show prompts Travers to wonder less at the parade of canines, than at the preoccupations of their owners, whom she labels "half-and-half creature(s), Calibans of Olympia, mid-way between dog and man" (28 October 1937). If the image of a myopic subspecies totally absorbed in canine lore is prominent in the denizens of the dog show, metaphors of an underwater life aptly convey Travers' judgement of the chromium-plated plutocracy of the motor show. She has real fun with this "briny atmosphere . . . of life under the wave" (3 November 1938), because every one of her marine comparisons heightens the sense of unreality and vulgarity on display. "Heavy and solid and bright-finned as Atlantic pollock," shiny limousines swim toward the crowd. "Salesmen like sea-anemones thrust out tentacle arms"; the less energetic hucksters are simply "dried herring." As an overwrought escapee, swimming down "the foggy brine-lit alleys to the exit," Travers finds new comfort in her old car with the dented mudguard, the slit canvas hood, the hole in the carpet, and the bent nail in the door. A similar gratitude—partly relieved and partly rueful—for a return to the familiar round is evident in her accounts of a picnic in the French Alps and a strange encounter in the London underground. At the opening of "Picnic in the Snow" (24 March 1938), when describing the departure for "Notre Dame de B―― ――," Travers anticipates the marvellous: "the sleighs, already gaudy with painted stars, sprout tall spears of mimosa as though Spring had overtaken them in the night," an allusion which could remind readers of the Nellie–Rubina episode in *Mary Poppins Comes Back* (1935), when spring literally does come overnight. Her chance meeting of a shabby looking character in the underground station called Angel (which, almost half a century later, is the locale for another bizarre encounter in Salman Rushdie's *The Satanic Verses*) is a more unnerving episode. This 'person,' "wings humped on his bowed shoulders" and talking of his "father's mansions," is clearly not of the earthly realm (13 June 1940). Despite his derelict appearance he has sobering words for those who think that work and productivity are curealls. "'Strange, isn't it—very strange that nobody has any time? Time is their element, they eat and drink it. Their bodies are hung on bones of time. . . . And yet, their ceaseless cry is "No time, no time!"'" His point strikes home for the reviewer who, curiously enough, in missing the station which has been her regular access to the theatre district, has not completed her assignment, but has seen "the sky's engulfing and effulgent light" anew in the wings of this "solitary figure." It does not seem too far-fetched to suggest that Travers' ruminations on this figure later resulted in the Tramp–Angel in the "Every Goose a Swan" chapter of *Mary Poppins in the Park* (1952), who unsettles illusions, puts characters in "awkward predicaments," and finally flutters away as "a tattered scrap between his lifting wings."[3]

Travers' Irish heritage is prominent in some occasional essays, too. Although she often writes at great length about the Irish character, the influence of the sea, even in the bosky inlands, and the unique aspects of light "striking the rock," she vehemently opposes the "Anglo-American conception of the Irishman as romantic" (2 September 1937). In contrast, she stresses the qualities of realism and resilience, the results, in her estimate, of the particular geography and outlook of Ireland. The lights and abundance of Dublin, which she reports on during the London blackout, remind her of the suitability that "according to law . . . England, like a martial husband, should ride out to battle and . . . Ireland should stay at home keeping house for poetry and first principles" (16 November 1939).

Travers' various reactions to wartime existence—her three-part essay, "Our Village," on its effects in a small Sussex community; the twelve installments of her "Letters from Another World," reporting scenes of political life in North America; and other, more intermittent essays—all attempt to relate the losses, disruptions, and fears to some form of earthly rhythm. Her first account of the blackout welcomes this "ancient recreating fountain of darkness," this return to "an old heritage," in which the city "swings now to earth's rhythm, goes with the sun and calmly obeys the law" (19 October 1939). A similar faith in natural laws and resilience lies behind her reports on the effects of Hitler, air raids, and the influx of evacuees on the village identified only as "M———": "the village has its roots in earth. It is part of the ancient order of things and so will stand secure" (26 October 1939). By the time of the final essay, however, her tone is less bluff and more clearly determined to outlast the devastation; furthermore, as this poignant exchange with a soldier who had once been her gardener illustrates, Travers' attitude toward all forms of growth and life has become increasingly pragmatic.

> The war is changing us. My one-time gardener, shipped home from France after a series of Crusoe-like adventures, limped the three large miles from the village to see me. After hearing his story we took a ceremonious turn in the garden. Nervously, remembering his old relentless vigilance, I apologized for the daisies and clover on the lawn. He regarded them gently, gazing long and quietly as one looks at a long-loved friend. 'Dainty! That's what they are,' he said, graciously. 'Let them bide!' Then to cover the lapse he spat vigorously, but I was not taken in. After living cheek to cheek with slaughter a man likes to see things grow and live, even the changelings. (15 August 1940)

The decision of the neighboring market town to proceed with its Bank Holiday Fair is another source of comfort; the main appeal for Travers is the merry-go-round with its blurring of perspectives, "a journey to some country lying alongside, perhaps *within* this world, unknown but guessed at, infinitely desirable." Signif-

icantly, in this last contribution before she embarks for America,
Travers emphasizes the importance of the very mechanism—the
merry-go-round—by which Mary Poppins whirled out of the lives
of the Banks children at the end of *Mary Poppins Comes Back*
(1935). She does this with an explanation of "setting out upon a
journey" which fits both Travers' own situation and that of the
elusive nanny: ". . . [T]he landscape we knew so well when we
were still upon the ground becomes unfamiliar and exciting, the
outward lineament of that unknown inside world."

Travers' letters from America represent another sort of exploration, less an inward spiralling than comparative assessment of
American reaction to the growing threat of war, in light of her
British experience. Clearly the blackouts and rationings have had
long lasting effects: she admits feeling "uneasy at night with bare
lights and shining streets" (26 December 1940), and "famished"
(20 March 1941) when she beholds the abundance of fruits, veg-
etables, and cheeses in shop windows. Travers' ship docks in Hal-
ifax; she travels by train to Montreal and then by plane to New
York. Although the diary account of this passage in *I Go by Sea,
I Go by Land* is quite lyrical, she hints of exhaustion and exas-
peration when she observes that "it takes an angel or a deaf-mute
to travel on a ship evacuating private and government children
and remain equable at the end of the voyage" (26 December 1940).
After such candor a Canadian reader can almost forgive her labeling Nova Scotia a dry "state." Her most illuminating reportage
is the letter about Pearl Harbor, in which she watches the steady
accumulation of horrific detail dismantle American confidence
and experiences an outsider's "kind of weary pity to hear the same
phrases coming up again here" (22 December 1941). As "moment
by moment" the wireless gives out "more terrible news, all the
more harrowing for the over-confident commentaries inter-
spersed between bulletins," the announcers' bravado that "Japan
would be licked before Christmas" fails to convince. Yet her account of the roll-call in both the Congress and the Senate the next
day, preceding the declaration of war, expresses dread and fear of
the U.S. response to aggression, conveniently forgetting the British reaction to German aggression just two years before. "It

seemed to me in no sense a gathering of men but a den of lions and lions waiting to be fed. As each man's name was called he answered, not with a human voice, but with a low deep snarling 'Ay!' that was straight from the jungle."

Upon her return from America, Travers catalogued "the richness and the strangeness" she had experienced on both sides of the Atlantic in this reverse sea-change:

> America—mentally, emotionally, physically—tightens, sharpens, makes dry and sparkling; braces, takes measurements, asks everything, waits for nobody; is hard with a soft centre; has, as her element, sky; is frosty, arid, friendly, lonely; runs west, with the wind in the east. England—threaded through with the west wind and the inlets of the sea—relaxes, unloosens; makes no demand and asks no questions; is without curiosity; has, as her element, earth; is moist, heavy and intimate— soft, but firm at the core; sluggish, forever waiting, half-asleep on her feet at the cross-roads. (27 September 1945)

She admits that these are "first impressions, capable of being reversed at any moment." Since she is just beginning to feel the full effects of homesickness, after having been transplanted for five years, her willingness to reverse herself as she becomes reacquainted with England is understandable. Yet this tenuous, emotional groping represents a considerable shift from the precise, assured voice that characterizes most of her theater criticism. Her work for children, composed during the stay in America and reflecting the realities of early postwar Britain, is more revealing of her divided affections and loyalties.

4

Wartime Evacuation:
Fact as Fable

Like all those who are very young I had made the
mistake of thinking that there are separate rivers of
life and death. Now I knew that there is only one
tide, whole and indivisible.
                                    —*Ah Wong,* 1943

Travers' stories composed and published during her wartime
years are all, in various ways, attempts at reintegration, harmony, and peace. Though separated by both time and geography,
she devotes three of her four Christmas and New Year's gift books
to reminiscences of her Australian childhood. The other gift book,
Happy Ever After, which is the first draft of a chapter from *Mary
Poppins Opens the Door* (1943), charmingly permits a benign and
extended glance at the few seconds when "all things are at one."[1]
Both of the other books from this period employ the voice of the
child, as diarist or questioner, to comment on the fractures and
fresh starts effected by the war. There is nothing escapist or nos-
talgic about her wartime writing. In essence it is heartening and
courageous, viewing the present as part of a larger, richer continuum of events, influences, and symbols.

The three gift books recalling aspects of her childhood, *Aunt
Sass* (1941), *Ah Wong* (1943), and *Johnny Delaney* (1944), tell as
much about Travers, the responsible, sensitive, eldest child, as
about the relatives and household employees who are their osten-

sible subjects. The maternal great aunt, Christina Saraset, left an indelible impression on Travers even before the family came to live with her. "Stern and tender, secret and proud, anonymous and loving," Aunt Sass, a spinster and, in some ways, a holy terror, was planted firmly as a figure of importance and authority in Travers' family, "like the central shaft of a merry-go-round."[2] Born in Australia in 1846, Aunt Sass was the eldest of a large Victorian family of emigré British parents. This "ancestress and matriarch" (10) is fondly and wittily remembered in the memoir, which was composed a year after her death at the age of ninety-four.

At the outset, Travers establishes that the enchanting feature of this remarkable person was the discrepancy between outside and inside, appearance and reality. "Imagine a bulldog whose ferocious exterior covers a heart tender to the point of sentimentality and you have Christina Saraset" (5). Although Aunt Sass's authoritarianism is undeniable—in her "pithy tracts of moral behaviour and solid fact" from which "right and wrong" emerged as her "favourite subjects" (7), in her recounting of historical events "simply as a background for her own life" (7), and in her issuing of orders "as though she were a general at the War Office and spit-spot, off you went, trembling, to carry them out or perish" (15)—her grand niece sensed more delight than terror in her presence. Admiration for Aunt Sass's bizarre lore shines throughout this memoir. Her historical facts, for instance, which seemed on first hearing to be "equally piquant and irrelevant" (8), later impress Travers as sound and illuminating. Aunt Sass's decidedly odd account of guests carrying their own bread to dinner parties begins to make gradual sense.

> . . . [T]he vision of Aunt Sass setting out for Government House, all lace and taffeta, with a loaf of bread under one arm, ceased to be funny. Brooding over her reminiscences I realised that in those days the clearings in the bush must still have been small and scanty. Much time and energy are necessary to make wattle and eucalyptus give way to wheat and rye. Bread, therefore, must have been infinitely precious. (9)

The rumbling voice and ominously snapping eyes which accompanied her directives never paralyzed Travers. Aunt Sass often added the fillip of a sudden twist to nursery rhymes, which appealed to the child as "more exciting than the known or expected rhythm." Travers remembers these emendations to a traditional ditty and to Hoffman's mock-cautionary verse:

> *Little Bo-Peep has lost her sheep*
> *And can't tell where to find them,*
> *Leave them alone and they'll come home*
> *Saying* "What a thoroughly careless little girl!"
> . . .
> *Augustus was a chubby lad,*
> *Fat ruddy cheeks Augustus had*
> *And everybody saw with joy*
> The disgustingly overfed unhealthy-looking child!
> (16)

This on-the-spot limericist is nevertheless hectoring and opinionated, treasuring "a profound conviction that all women—with the single exception of herself—were wrong and all men splendidly right" (20). The first meal of the recently bereaved family, who has just traveled the 700 miles to live with Aunt Sass, is a momentous affair in which this "sargeant" (25), descants "unfavourably on [their] table manners, upbringing, personal appearance and ghastly features" (26), and succeeds in driving everyone from the room in tears except Travers. The confrontation between these two strong minded individuals is actually the prelude to Aunt Sass's crusty, but affectionate and trusting, patronage.

> "And now, I suppose, *you'll* break down and go, too!" she
> said jeeringly, taking the last handful of cherries.
> "I will not, you old Beast!" I shouted to her. "I'm not
> crying, it's only my eyes!"
> At that I saw the light kindle in the fierce old face, a
> leaping joy at finding an adversary that would stand up
> to her and not give one inch of ground.

"Here," she said, "take the cherries to the little ones
and tell your Mother Aunt Sass is a bitter old woman and
that she didn't mean a word of it." (26)

Having journeyed between Australia and England seventeen
times, and "amassed unlimited friends and memories" in both
countries (12), Aunt Sass established herself as an arbiter of taste
and culture, whom no one dared defy, and for whom the writing
of her reminiscences seemed "so vulgarly disrespectful" (13). The
gift book is a tribute to this woman whose snappishness never
fooled Travers for a moment. "I know you, Christina Saraset—
you naked and vulnerable inside the horny armour!" (29). Back-
grounds, terrains, overland journeys, and all other figures fade to
insignificance in this single character study. As the seasoned
storyteller and reviewer, deftly assembling episodes and remarks
to promote the impression of well concealed kindness, Travers appears considerably less vulnerable, more self-aware in *Aunt Sass*
than in other gift books. She tantalizes the reader with the
tossed-off observation that her subject may be found "occasionally
in the pages of 'Mary Poppins'" (32)—a comment which suggests
a bevy of diverse characters, from Miss Andrew and Miss Lark,
to the censorious nanny herself, in whom some of Christina
Saraset's traits may have been sprinkled as germinating seeds.

The narrator's voice in *Ah Wong* and *Johnny Delaney* seems
less guarded, mainly because the personages recalled, the
Chinese cook, Ah Wong, and the Irish handyman and ex-jockey,
Johnny Delaney, are figures of such unequivocal sympathy and
affection. Though these men are attached to the children, both
are loners, and though the celebration of Christmas is a prominent feature in the interrelated books, neither hero has any patience with institutional religion or church going. To prove his
conclusion that "church pretty silly stuff, I tink-im," Ah Wong ex-
patiates—with the Cantonese inflections so characteristic of all
his speech—on the apparently nonsensical ritual of the collection.
"'What! Money on a plate! You put puddings on a plate, or lamb
chops. . . . Whassa dam-silly fellow nonsins. . . . And where I get-
im money, hey? Ah Wong bin big-mob poor chap—no gotta no

money!"[3] It is worth noting that while Travers' penchant for reproducing dialects has resulted in criticism of her racial stereotypes in *Mary Poppins* (see Chapter Six), no comment has been made about the potentially racist implications of Ah Wong's speech patterns. The general inaccessibility of this gift book could provide a cynical explanation; a more fitting one, I think, takes into account the love for this figure and reverence of his inscrutable oriental ways, which motivate the narrator at every turn. For his part, Johnny angrily avoids religious topics and encounters: "The mere sight of a priest enraged him; and he deliberately pressed his hat a little further on his head when he met Mr. Preston, the Vicar."[4] Yet, he and Ah Wong lead deeply spiritual private lives, which create lasting, reverberative impressions in the children's "inmost hearts and spirits," and lift their lives "from their dull round into a kind of legend" (*Johnny Delaney,* 18).

Although the cook, who offers the seasonal salute "'Melly Clismus,'" only manages this mangled version of a Christmas carol:

> Hark, de helald angels singe-ee
> Gloly to de newbone king-ee
> Peace on earth and mercymile
> Goddam sinners reconsile, (14)

Travers' memoir of such a beloved figure is truly a reconciliation of past and present. Years after her father's death when the family had been forced to leave the plantation, the narrator, now a cub reporter, is assigned to interview the captain of a battered cargo ship, carrying old men back to China to die. She is greeted by Ah Wong's familiar voice in the close and grimly packed hold. Hearing "'Big-fellow Little Missy'" (21) carries her back to her "earliest elements." "The green fronds of cane were about me, the smells of the hold mingled with the scent of incense in Ah Wong's room on the plantation" (21). Taking his frail hands in her own, she understands in a new way the "living stream" that connects them, for "the same flood that was flinging me into life was taking Ah Wong home" (23).

The discernment and avuncular gentleness that were part of Johnny Delaney were apparent to the narrator even as a child. As well as boarding the horses and teaching the children to ride, Johnny was a shrewd observer of his employers. Travers remembers the comments of this normally taciturn man on the death of her mother's uncle, whom Johnny labels an "'ould divil'"; "'Well, our lives'll be brighter without him, if he hasn't embezzled yer trust funds'" (9). Johnny's brogue and taunting meiosis do not conceal the fact that Travers' family was left so straitened, after the sudden death of her father, because of this uncle's thievery. Despite his avoidance of clergy and church, Johnny's "life work" (28) is an exceptional, carved and painted, creche scene, which the children discover close to his bedside after his death on Christmas Eve. "No shepherds with flocks of snowy lambs, no angels with folded wings. Instead there were little native creatures—kangaroos, emus, red flamingoes; horses and lizards and goats. The kneeling men were cane-cutters, offering green cane boughs; swagmen with blankets rolled on their shoulders; drovers carrying whips in their hands and their steers standing meekly by" (32). The crowned figures, appropriately, consisted of likenesses of Travers' father, Ah Wong (whose name means "King"), and Billy Pee-Kow, a black cane-cutter, whom Johnny had befriended. Four children, "recognisably ourselves," were represented in blue smocks, and standing alone and apart was "a little bowed hump-backed figure with a jockey-cap in its hand." Significantly, too, the narrator, whom Johnny had defended as "black with loving," recognizing "in her coils of passion" the individual "going forward against the thorn, who needs to be treasured and cared for" (17), puts the final touch on his work; she convinces her mother not to bury Johnny with the unattached part of his scene. She removes the halo from his hand and clicks home the golden ring, "neatly, firm and sure" on the child in the manger (32). This concluding detail aptly crystallizes the bond between these two special adults and the children, which is the shared topic of these privately printed Christmas greetings.

Travers' first seasonal gift book to appear, *Happy Ever After*, was published as a New Year's greeting, and was a draft of the

penultimate chapter of the third Mary Poppins book, *Mary
Poppins Opens the Door*. The description of the precious seconds,
between the first and last strokes of midnight, which herald the
beginning of the new year is, in itself, revealing of Travers' long-
standing preoccupation with reconciliation. In the crack, between
the old year and the new, "the eternal opposites lie down together—the wolf and the lamb, the young and the old, the shining
poles, the night and the day—and the circle is complete" (19). Although the story reads like a spontaneous combination of the lyricism of Isaiah (especially 11. 6–9) with the finale of a fairy tale,
it is as carefully plotted as all Mary Poppins' escapades. This fact
becomes even clearer when the gift book version is compared with
the changes Travers introduced for the final draft of the book,
providing a unique glimpse of the author as editor of her own
work.

Both versions open and close in the nursery of the Banks household, with the children being tucked into bed on New Year's Eve
at the outset, and awakening to New Year's Day at the conclusion.
Mary Poppins engages in the same formulaic denials of any fantastic celebration in both accounts, just as the children discover
and connive at her secret. In both they are treated to her pithy
dictum, that their future happiness depends on them. The
changes in the final version involve a sharpening of focus and an
addition of details to clarify the emphasis on concord and the
union of opposites, which becomes increasingly frenzied as time
runs out. While Travers' feelings of uprootedness and homesickness may have been inducements to the themes of harmony and
peace, the time between these two versions, (probably about two
years), allowed her to supply more pointed cues about the form
and meaning of the story. When, in *Happy Ever After*, Michael
Banks dares to ask what happens between the first and last
stroke at midnight, Mary Poppins snaps priggishly, "'Curiosity
killed the Cat!'" (6). Momentarily fearless, Michael wades in even
deeper with the retort, "'But I'm not a cat. I'm a boy and I want
to know'" (7). In the penultimate chapter, Mary Poppins' sniffing
reply is actually a rhetorical question, "'Do you think I'm a Mind
Reader?,'" to which a timorous Michael, who "wanted to say Yes,

for that was exactly what he did think, . . . never dare[d]"[5] to react. While Mary Poppins herself is more a retailer of adages in the final version—cautioning her charges not to "trouble Trouble till Trouble troubles you" and leaping to the conclusion that "Want must be [Michael's] Master" (176)—it is the children's cautious silences and conjectures that forecast the way matters will unfold. Travers includes Jane more prominently in the book version; this astute oldest child is the observer of the exchange with Michael who wonders "to herself" why Mary Poppins had set their "well-known books," *Robinson Crusoe, The Green Fairy Book,* and *Mother Goose Nursery Rhymes,* in front of the four toy animals she had just reclaimed from the children: "Does she mean the animals to read the books?" (179).

Although the roster of reanimated and strangely affectionate fairy tale and nursery rhyme characters differs in each text, the most discernible change between the New Year's romp of *Happy Ever After,* where Michael observes in amazement that "everything is different" (18), and in *Mary Poppins Opens the Door,* where he finds it all "upside down" (188), is the hope and fragility of these reunions in the later version. Travers not only provides more details about the happy meeting of Cock Robin and Jenny Wren; Red Riding Hood "hugging" the Wolf (188); Miss Muffet gently patting the Spider; Jack and the Giant as "bosom friends" (190); and the Farmer's Wife "dancing with Three Blind Mice" (195); but she also pauses thoughtfully to comment on—and drive home the point of—the rare moment when music and dance unite the whole scene. "Everybody had a partner. No one was lonely or left out. All the fairy tales ever told were gathered together on that square of grass, embracing each other with joy" (195–196). Travers' emphasis on the drama of this tenuous reunion is evident in the change in description of the tenth stroke, from "Ten! The grass was swaying and waving beneath the thundering feet" (24), to "Ten! O Lion and Unicorn, Wolf and Lamb! Friend and Enemy! Dark and Light!" (197). The verbs conveying the end of this pastoral vision ("broke and scattered," "streamed away and seemed to melt," "dissolved into the air") are identical in both versions, but the way in which Travers returns the action to Cherry

Tree Lane is significantly different. In the earlier draft, she simply deposits the reader after the music dies away and a pealing of bells "from every tower and steeple, . . . clear and loud and triumphant," takes its place (24). In the later text, she transports the reader with nursery rhyme geography (possibly playing on the tune of "Oranges and Lemons"): "The fairy-tale music died away, it was lost in the lordly peal of bells. For now from every tower and steeple the chimes rang out, triumphant. Big Ben, St. Paul's, St. Bride's, Old Bailey, Southwark, St. Martin's, Westminster, Bow" (199). As the Opies' scholarship in *The Oxford Dictionary of Nursery Rhymes* clarifies,[6] the rhyme's provenance and association with games of tug-of-war and square-for-eight dancing suggest that this coda might actually throw into relief the themes of the preceding interlude. Travers eases the transition from "in the crack" to awaking in bed, making it less abrupt, by adding another adjective to describe the beckoning tingle of the Crumpet Man's bell in the street below, which wakes the children. As well as being "familiar and nearer home," his ting-aling-aling is now also "friendly."

The circular completeness of Mary Poppins' escapades is not available to Travers, when she relies on an eleven-year-old diarist as the storyteller in *I Go by Sea, I Go by Land*. With her acute ear for the speech patterns of a 1940's British preadolescent and sympathetic affiliation with the sensitive, artistic older child, Travers allows Sabrina Lind to recount her own experiences and feelings, crossing the Atlantic and living in America for the remainder of the war. Sabrina journeys with her nine-year-old brother James, in the company of a family friend identified only as "Pel." This woman, who is a writer, carries with her a baby boy in a basinette; Romulus, one assumes, could be Pel's child. The children are making the crossing to stay with their mother's childhood friend, Harriet Seaton, and Harriet's husband George.

Although this diary has a predictable diffuseness, Travers attempts narrative cohesion through the use of traditional hymns, "Matthew, Mark, Luke and John, / Bless the bed that I lie on . . ." and "Now the day is over, / Night is drawing nigh . . . ," as epigraph and postscript. These lyrical bookends encase the diary of a dislocated girl within a theological framework of hope, comfort, and protection. As the evening prayer used for the epigraph makes clear, Travers borrowed her title directly from this source.

> I go by sea, I go by land,
> The Lord made me with His right hand.
> If any danger come to me,
> Sweet Jesus Christ deliver me.

Even the hymn's origin, in Thomas Ady's collection, *A Candle in the Dark* (1656), which employed practical logic along with religious convictions to combat popular superstitions about stargazing and witchcraft, supports the diary's overall sense of trust in a benign providence. This trust is reiterated in the famous Victorian berceuse of the Squarson (squire–parson) of the remote parish of Lew Trenchard in Devon, Sabine Baring–Gould (1834–24). Sabrina chooses it to sing James to sleep because, for the girl, it is "the only song I know that says everything."[7] Fittingly, children and sailors are specific beneficiaries of divine guardianship.

> Grant to little children
> Visions bright of thee.
> Guard the sailors tossing
> On the deep blue sea.

Pel's presence is itself reassuring, but the adjustment to separation from parents and village friends and to life in another country falls on the diarist. Appropriately, too, Travers reproduces the orthography and chatty, self important style of this girl, who consistently refers to her work as a "Dairy," and seems addicted to capitalizing. Sabrina tries hard to abide by her father's counsel about the two important things: "Love and Courrage [*sic*]" (25). Despite her resolve, the child's thoughts often return to her village, under the pseudonym of "Thornfield," and to her mother, left alone when her father entered the services. Travers'

obsession with concealing private, personal, autobiographical details relaxes when she lets Sabrina write about the universal feelings of loneliness and anxiety.

> . . . I looked at James and knew that we were both think-
> ing of Thornfield. Oh, what are they all doing now?
> Mother will be quite alone tonight. She will be sitting in
> the big white chair in the study with Mouse (who is a cat
> not a mouse) on her knee and she will have her folded
> away brooding look that makes her seem so small and
> loveable. She will be thinking of us out on the sea. And
> here we are not even moving. There is no way of telling
> her not to think of us on the sea and be anxious. We can-
> not get to her anywhere. O dear darrling! I have told
> James we will have hot baths tonight. When you have a
> hot bath everything changes and is smoothed out and
> perhaps tonight we won't remember so much when we go
> to bed. (39)

One of the most charming aspects of the diary is its believable
characterization of the Lind children as two distinct individuals.
Sabrina's maternal instincts are already well developed, as evidenced not only in her tender care of James, who is "still so
young" (70), and her interest in the baby born to the neighbors of
the Eastons, but also in Pel's assessment of Sabrina who, like the
eldest child in the later *Johnny Delaney,* has "a full cup", and
must "learn to carry it without spilling over" (69). Sabrina wants
to put down deep and lasting roots, "to stay still in one place for
a long time like a plant coming up every year" (140). James, by
contrast poetic and mercurial, seems initially to enjoy change, yet
still strives to unite past and present, known and unknown.
Among his ditties recorded in his sister's diary, my own favorite
is this transAtlantic composition devoted to domesticating or
taming some of the cosmic, transcendent mysteries of human life.

> If I had a star
> Out of the sky

I'd light a fire with it
To make toast by.

If I had a moon
I'd hang it on a tree
And cover it with leaves
So it couldn't see me.

If I had an angel
With a blue wing
I'd sit him on the mantelpiece
And make him sing. (77)

This poet also stores many memories, from his childhood and even from a prenatal state, reminiscent of Annabel Banks in *Mary Poppins Comes Back,* who remembers in the cradle her "long journey" from "where all things have their beginning."[8] As James dictates to Sabrina:

. . . I remember Mrs. Leeves' home-made ginger-ale
And helping Jim dig the Marigolds
In the Bottom Meadow.
I remember the Hop Fields
Like dark green tunnels
And stamping the hops into the pig-bags
To make them tighter.
I remember the Gypsy singing
"Ero, the lovely man
That went to Galway riding a drake,"
And the Rat Hole under the bread oven
And the place where the Hen Pheasant built her nest
Close to the nut hedge
With seventeen young ones.
I remember everything,
There is nothing I do not remember
Ever since I was born
And even before. (119–20)

Travers' ability to remember seems to be as agile as James's, for she adds certain telltale details to Sabrina's descriptions that hint of her own Australian childhood. The son of the Seatons' chauffeur, who comes from County Clare, teaches the children "the Long Spit, the Drop Spit and the Over-the-Shoulder" (112), recalling the exact spitting tricks Johnny Delaney taught Travers and her siblings (*Johnny Delaney* 21). Mr. Seaton's Great Aunt Porter, judgemental and wrinkled, bears an uncanny likeness to Travers' Aunt Sass.

Although the diary trails off not long after James's tenth birthday, the prospects for the children's fitting into American life, for as long as they remain, are reasonably good. They do not, of course, renounce an iota of middle class Anglophilia in the process, and only gradually allow themselves to be called refugees instead of evacuees, because they are certain that their American friends "know now we are not Poles or Belgians in soup kitchens" (177). Sabrina's observation on a history lesson in her new school encapsulates the changes in perspective and location, with which she grapples throughout the diary. "When we do History at home America seems a very small spot in the corner of your mind. But here it is the other way round and England is the very small spot" (206).

The unifying motifs of the gift books, and Travers' many attempts to thread characters, details, and questions from her own past into the wartime stories, perhaps reach their consummation in *The Fox at the Manger,* her account of the first postwar Christmas Eve carol service at St. Paul's. Though published in 1963, this narrative of her afternoon adventure with three little boys, whom she takes to the cathedral, is clearly set in the London of 1945. The first person authorial voice deftly and professionally controls the design, which is tidier for the almost two decades separating the book from the event. But the story, with the careful choreography of the inserted Bewick woodcuts, loses nothing in immediacy and freshness of dialogue.

An affective meditation on gift giving, *The Fox at the Manger* leaps over historical periods in the conviction that "all time, all space is one . . . and nothing is incongruous."[9] Travers identifies this outlook as part of the "strict and fixed" (70) laws of childhood: "Two thousand years ago is now, fact and fable are both true and nothing separates them" (71). The actions and questions of the three children trigger the exploration. Travers only labels her companions X. Y. and Z., but her disclosure, "one near and dear to me, and the others his best friends" (25), suggests that they may have been the child "Romulus" (having outgrown the basinette of *I Go by Sea, I Go by Land*) and his friends. The boys are each planning to donate an old toy to the poor children, as a traditional part of this carol service. The shabby lion "whose one remaining eye hung by a thread" (26), the toy bus with chipped paint, and the tailless, rubber mouse prove too precious to give up however, and the unashamed trio zigzag toward the front pew, "their bodies bulging with the ungiven gifts" (31). These nondonors are nonetheless very precise and forthright observers. One remarks that the smooth grey donkey at the manger does not meet the requirements of the shaggy, brown gift giver in the "Carol of the Friendly Beasts," another comments that the vested clergymen look like Wee Willie Winkie in nightgowns, and the third whispers audibly that the bishop is not singing but mouthing the words. These comments prompt Travers' own observations about inadequacy. The rose-bloom faces in the creche scene and the absence of a black lamb cause her to "want more, especially for the children's sake" (22). In addition to "faces trodden by crows'-feet, signs of ferment, . . . something of life, even in the carven faces, someone out of breath with running, someone stricken with joy," she "dearly" wants a black lamb. "For, without him, where are the ninety and nine? Flocks, like families, have need of their black sheep—he carries their sorrow for them. He is the other side of their whiteness. Does nobody understand, I wondered, that a crib without a black lamb is an incomplete statement?" (22). The honesty and completeness of Johnny Delaney's carving may have flashed through Travers' mind as she sat in the pew.

In fact, childhood memories along with children's directness play an important part in *The Fox at the Manger*. The narrator is flummoxed by an insistent "'Why'" from one of her companions, questioning the need for him to remove his cap while Travers wears a hat. This serves as the prelude for her return to a family pew scene in her own childhood. As often as the young Travers drapes her new blue sash across her stomach, her exasperated mother jerks it back "into its proper place" (33). This seesaw continues until the mother finally hisses "'It's not *supposed* to be worn like that!'" and the child counters with "'Why not?'" Patience and logic exhausted, the mother retreats into her own reverie: "So *she* pretended not to hear and for self-protection floated off to sit beside *her* mother. And soon, perhaps, she, too, said 'Why?' and her mother floated swiftly away; and then *her* mother, and then and then—" (33). Yet such a retreat is not really an infinite regress of fictions. It is, as I see it, integrally related to the structure of this story, which itself returns for half of its length to an imagined and distant past around the original manger.

The Fox at the Manger is actually a fable about giving, totality and loss, union and comradeship. As X's query, "'Why weren't there any *wild* animals at the crib?'" (39), initiates the shift, the London setting of the first half gives way to the manger scene of the second, in which the fox offers his gift of cunning to the Child. Despite the accusations of the other animals—recalling in some ways the rough justicers of La Fontaine's "Les Animaux Malades de la Peste" (*Fables, Book* VII, 1)—the fox proceeds. His own explanation of his name, *Raginohardus* meaning "'strong in counsel'" (47), balances neatly with his "good" and "whole" (56) gift to the Child, who thus becomes "'the fox now, alone against the world'" (61).

The symmetry of gifts given and ungiven, uniting the halves, is reflected in the fable's epigraph and epilogue. As her opening, Travers chooses the anonymous French "Carol of the Friendly Beasts," in which donkey, cow, sheep, and dove are all mild, domestic gift givers, and closes with the forecasted union of the fox, from the manger of two thousand years ago, with the wild swan, whom the children sight winging her way along the Mall. An additional balance of desires emerges from the two parts of the story. The London section climaxes with the "melodious outcry" of the Christmas bells in which Travers hears *"concord, harmony, unison, peace!"* (37). The stable scene closes quietly with her vision of "barnyard beasts lying down with the fox," since "everything must be whole" (65). In these instances, Travers seems to underscore the hopes and insights she nursed throughout the wartime period.

5

The Conundrum of Mary Poppins:
Real *Wherever* She Happens to Be

"But tell me, Mary Poppins," begged Jane, as she
looked from the coloured picture-book to the confi-
dent face above her. "Which are the children in the
story—the Princes, or Jane and Michael?"

Mary Poppins was silent for a moment. She
glanced at the children on the printed page and back
to the living children before her. Her eyes were as
blue as the Unicorn's, as she took Jane's hand in
hers.

They waited breathlessly for her answer.
            —*Mary Poppins in the Park,* 1952

For all her propriety and tidiness, Mary Poppins is the quintes-
sential shapeshifter. As efficiently as she orders the nursery
world at 17 Cherry Tree Lane, this extraordinary nanny celebrates—with an insider's élan—a series of gay, dithyrambic
events. These unpredictable episodes, skewing the conventions of
time and space, and happily suspending the disbelief of her young
charges, show not just one side but several differing facets of the
unique and talented heroine. At home in both a domestic reality
and a mythic universe, this enigma outwits all attempts to pin
her down.

To appreciate her sparkling graces means to accept incongrui-
ties and mysteries. With her woodendoll features, contemptuous

sniffs, and tart rebuffs, she is the controlling yet ultimately inexplicable force in the Banks household. Every member of the community is subjected to her smugness; she flummoxes Mrs. Banks, reduces Jane and Michael to instant penitence or fearful silence, and leaves ordinarily gregarious shopkeepers stammering and diffident. But the children cling to her hard, bony body more often out of veneration than for protection. This curt and censorious figure is also, on occasion, an enchanting storyteller. Her voice, which can be icicle sharp, communicates with animals (wild and domestic), babies, toys, constellations, mythical characters, the Sun, and the Moon. Her eyes not only catch the pleasing reflection of her own new hats, shoes, gloves, and handbags, but also penetrate the depths of the children's thoughts. The welcoming smell of newly-made toast hangs about Mary Poppins, but her fixity and sense of purpose also make her an imposing pillar of starch. Proud of never wasting time with officious bumpkins like the Park Keeper, she has relatives who float in the air, turn Catherine wheels, whirl atop music boxes, and emerge from plasticene blobs. After each extraordinary escapade, like rolling and bobbing airborne during afternoon tea, waltzing with the Sun, or conversing with a unicorn, she flatly denies any connection with the fantastic. But her sympathies are easily engaged—for the poor Match-man who cannot afford an outing, the scantily clad star on a Christmas shopping spree, the transplanted court jester who appears to be an indolent man-of-no-work, and the marble statue longing for some human companionship. Although Mary Poppins defies understanding or explanation, the victims of her quick tongue label her with such tags as the Misfit, Caliban, or wolf in sheep's clothing. The more discerning characterizations come from those who revel in her remarkable metamorphosing powers; for them and for millions of readers—in twenty-five languages—she lives as the Great Exception, the Marvellous Wonder, the Mind Reader, and the "glow-worm shining to show . . . the right way home."[1]

Travers' sextet of Mary Poppins books, with the appended quartet of bibelots, stretches over a period of fifty-four years of her life, and is the home and core of her writing. She has insisted repeatedly that she wrote them not for children but for all readers and, primarily, for herself—even remarking obliquely that *Mary Poppins* is the story of her life. Some elements in the books do correspond with the tidbits of biographical information Travers has disclosed about her childhood, her experience of nannies, and her own work in minding children. But she resolutely disclaims any part in inventing this heroine. Instead she characterizes herself as a mere intermediary, someone whom Mary Poppins brushed past, and who had the good luck and sense to catch the impression and put it down. Evidently, though, the need to please herself, to welcome the return visit of Mary Poppins to her consciousness, partly explains the preoccupation of this writer in her eighties with an apparently ageless nanny tending a family securely locked in the 1930s.

In this canon of Travers' Mary Poppins books, certain stages of development are observable—even though Travers herself maintains that Mary Poppins has not changed at all. The first four, *Mary Poppins* (1934, hereafter *MP*), *Mary Poppins Comes Back* (1935, *MPCB*), *Mary Poppins Opens the Door* (1943, *MPOD*), and *Mary Poppins in the Park* (1952, *MPIP*), form a solid unit. Chapters decrease in number, and increase in size proportionally, from twelve to ten to eight to six. Characters reappear and the list of Mary Poppins' eccentric relatives grows. The often playful and ironic interrelationship of chapters is clear, with such titles as "Miss Lark's Andrew" and "Miss Andrew's Lark," and "Bad Tuesday," "Bad Wednesday," and "Lucky Thursday." Scenes of wild, cosmic celebration, where rings and chains of dance climax the festivities, are common elements, too, in "Full Moon," "The Evening Out," "High Tide," and "Hallowe'en." Similar formulae for whirling in and out of situations and, at times, in "Balloons *and* Balloons" and "Peppermint Horses," above situations unite this quartet of books. Also recurring are Mary Poppins' formulaic denials of unseemly behavior, invariably followed by some sort of emblematic proof, a vestige of the fantastic episode visible in the domestic world. The schemes of shrews, like Miss Persimmon, Mrs. Clump, and Mrs. Mo, who harass Mary Poppins' blithe male relatives, usually backfire, but occasionally, as with Miss Tartlet, love overcomes peevishness. A concern for bringing Mary Poppins in and out of the picture plays a big role in the first three books, while the fourth is a series of discrete events which may have occurred at any time during her three visits.

The next four books, in order of publication, *Mary Poppins from A to Z* (1962, *MPAZ*), *Maria Poppina ab A ad Z* (1968, *MaPAZ*), *A Mary Poppins Story for Coloring* (1969, *MPSC*) and *Mary Poppins in the Kitchen* (1975, *MPIK*), are primarily diversions, recalling earlier events and previously introduced characters. The first is a charmingly alliterated, alphabetized summary; the second, a Latinized version; the third, a coloring book; and the fourth, a collection of standard Edwardian recipes featuring such substantial fare as Kedgeree, Lancashire Hot Pot, and Welsh Rarebit. Although, in light of the sextet, *MPAZ* and *MPIK* may appear to be mere diversions, they are sensible and unified. With an alliterated, illustrated vignette on each page, *MPAZ* not only marches through the alphabet in twenty-six installments, but also closes with Mary Poppins' end-of-the-day checking in the nursery, moving from Z to A, until "Mary Poppins, too, is Asleep." Although earlier in the quartet, Mary Poppins had sniffed "contemptuously" at Michael's question, "'What do you think I am? An Encyclopaedia? Everything from A to Z?'" (*MPCB* 158), three decades later in a more soporific, less harried, mood, she ponders the Alphabet, allowing that "'it embraces everything. . . . All that is or was or will be lies between A and Z.'"

The cookery book certainly allows for little nonsense or mayhem in the kitchen. When Mrs. Brill is called away to help her niece, Ellen is off nursing her perpetual cold, and Mr. and Mrs. Banks must go to Brighton. They all return at the end of the week to find that, under Mary Poppins' vigilant supervision, the children are well nourished and the kitchen is clean. The recipes, both alphabetized and indexed, are the result of Travers' collaboration with Maurice Moore-Betty, who apprenticed at the London Ritz and runs his own cooking school in New York.

Her most recent work, including *Mary Poppins in Cherry Tree Lane* (1982, *MPCTL*) and *Mary Poppins and the House Next Door* (1988, *MPHND*), is anything but a tiresome rehash. Incorporat-

ing many of the insights gleaned from Travers' continuing exploration of myth and fairy tale, these full-length stories, each
consisting of a single chapter, examine harmony and restitution,
while upholding the importance of the unresolved, unclosed
narrative.

Even at the outset of Mary Poppins' remarkable career, this
nanny stood out among others. Since Roger Lancelyn Green, in
Tellers of Tales, connects *Mary Poppins* and its sequels with John
Masefield's generally contemporaneous *The Midnight Folk* (1927)
and *The Box of Delights* (1935), because of their mingling of magic
and fantasy "with everyday life,"[2] it seems appropriate to begin
by exploring the great differences between the storytelling of
Masefield and Travers. In *The Midnight Folk,* an imaginative
young boy, Kay Harker, lives under the severe tutelage of his governess, the rigid Sylvia Daisy. With the help of animated toys,
talking chessmen, eye-opening pictures, size-changing potions,
and magic spells, Kay eventually discovers long lost treasure, and
exonerates the memory of his great grandfather, once accused of
the treasure's theft. Clashes between good and evil continue in
The Box of Delights and, significantly, Sylvia Daisy, now Mrs.
Pouncer, is part of the greedy gang, bent on acquiring an ancient
box thought to contain the alchemical lore of Ramon Lully and
Arnold of Todi. By this point Kay is a schoolboy who, while traveling home for the Christmas holidays, has been befriended by a
mysterious stranger and given a wonderful box with the capaci-
ties to shrink his size and propel his movements. The cruelty and
heartlessness of his onetime governess provide the main con-
trasts between this action-filled, almost frenetic dream–fantasy
and Mary Poppins' escapades. Of course, Mary Poppins is a
nanny, not a governess, without doubt the central figure, not a
peripheral irritant, in the quartet. Moreover, since Travers has
insisted that she not be categorized a children's writer, it is also
feasible to consider her nanny in comparison with the more conventional representations of these trusted old spinsters in contemporary literature, faithfully retained, in large measure,
because of their utter inconsequentiality. The nanny in Evelyn
Waugh's *A Handful of Dust* (1934) provides a dramatic contrast

with Travers' center stage character, not only because the old woman assigned to care for John Andrew Last, the young heir, is a tedious character without even a name and generally content with such noncommittal monosyllables as "'well, we'll see,'" but because she is definitely at the lower end of an all important hierarchy. When John Andrew blurts out that his nanny is "a silly old tart," the real gap between employer and employee becomes obvious. The homily which Anthony Last delivers to his son underscores the point.

> "Now listen, John. It was very wrong of you to call nanny a silly old tart. First, because it was unkind to her. Think of all the things she does for you every day."
>
> "She's paid to."
>
> "Be quiet. And secondly, because you were using a word which people of your age and class do not use. Poor people use certain expressions which gentlemen do not. You are a gentleman. . . . You must learn to speak like someone who is going to have these things and to be considerate to people less fortunate than you, particularly women. Do you understand?"[3]

Admittedly, not only the facelessness and social inferiority of Waugh's nanny contrast sharply with Travers' character, but also the huge differences between a novel on, as Waugh put it in his preface, "the theme of the betrayed romantic," and Travers' ecstatic celebration of the nursery world keep them apart, and contribute to Mary Poppins' singularity.

She does not correspond to other nannies in either literature or life. The habit of employing single or widowed women to tend to nursery aged children characterized upper middle class and upper class families, according to Jonathan Gathorne-Hardy, from the mid nineteenth century to 1939, at which point, he argues, the view of the child as a miniature adult was finally replaced by the general acceptance of modern theories of child psychology and development. Mary Poppins is totally unlike Compton Mackenzie's alcoholic terror in *Sinister Street* (1912), nor does she possess the "blood-red violence" of Curzon's Miss Paraman, or the "violet tenderness" of Churchill's Mrs. Everest.[4] Mary Poppins evades or inverts most of the traits which Gathorne-Hardy attributes to the nanny. Among those he enumerates are a haughtiness compensating for lower class origins, and often evidenced in appropriating the employer's name, and a tendency to either cruelty or gentleness in executing the roles of nurse, mother substitute, and, occasionally, sexual temptress and initiator. Mary Poppins always exhibits great pride in her well bred, albeit bizarre, relatives; her attitude towards the Banks parents is the farthest thing from sycophancy or obsequiousness. One almost has the idea that it is Mary Poppins who employs them. In addition, Mrs. Banks, however fluttery and ineffectual she may seem, is a present and concerned mother whom Mary Poppins never dreams of replacing. As for the matter of sexual initiation, the coy innocence of all the books makes it a ridiculous nonissue: Mr. Banks appears surprised and a little peeved at the birth of their fifth child, and Mary Poppins' own response to the Match-man is, at best, sisterly and sympathetic.

In the specific realm of children's literature, Mary Poppins is also unique and unparalleled as a nanny. Until her advent, governesses or tutors whose duty was the moral development of their charges were stock, but less and less heeded, figures in literature written for children. They could be combinations of sensibility and sternness, as in Sarah Fielding's Mrs. Teachum (*The Governess* [1749]) and Mary Wollstonecraft's Mrs. Mason (*Original Stories* [1788]). Their characteristics could range all the way from the unctuousness of Mrs. Sherwood's Mr. Dalben (*The History of Henry Milner* [1822–37]) to the fiendishness of Masefield's Sylvia Daisy. While frustration with the governess or guardian (mainly on account of her cruelty) rarely reaches the vengeance executed in Saki's chilling short story, "Sredni Vashtar," the general slowness and stolidity of these women dislodge them more and more from the center of the children's attention. Under the myopic eye or severe discipline of governesses youngsters—like Masefield's Kay Harker—learned to cultivate a rich, private, imaginative life. In the stories of E. Nesbit and Kenneth Grahame nursery-aged children roamed and had adventures without adult or Olympian disbelief or interruptions. Mary Poppins closes this widening gap. Here is a nanny whom children rush to obey! She enters the child's pastoral world and, rather than shattering illusions, joyously extends and encourages awareness. Neither a factotum nor a pious exemplar, she is not obsessed with moral dictates, nor is she above indulging in vanity. She makes entertainment and storytelling ways of accepting and perhaps understanding those difficult concepts of unity, paradox, and continuity which, for her, precede and transcend morality.

The world of the Mary Poppins books is not one of realism. Although Mr. Banks, who, appropriately, works in a bank (according to his children "cutting out pennies and shillings and half-crowns and threepenny-bits"[5]), complains periodically about the shortage of money, and Mrs. Banks frets over the chaos that follows Mary Poppins' inexplicable disappearances, the first allegiance of these books is not to the mundanities of household finances, but to a heightened reality, where childlike reasoning prevails and nothing is ever fixed. The incident with the Royal Doulton Bowl, in the "Bad Wednesday" chapter of *MPCB,* when an out of sorts Jane, tired of the responsibilities of being the eldest, angrily flings her paint box at the bowl, is an ideal example of such reality. Mary Shepard's first illustration of this painted object shows "three little boys . . . playing horses" (54), a precise example of a Royal Doulton "Series Ware," (which refers to a collection of different items: jugs, jars, bowls, plates, teapots depicting scenes or characters with a related theme). The Bowl's theme is number 17 in the "Pastimes" series, introduced in 1902 and withdrawn by 1932. Thus it is likely that the mantelpiece ornament could have been Mrs. Banks' christening present. In her study of this series ware, Louise Irvine identifies the bowl's full title: "Boys playing Scotch horses—'A rough colt can make the best horse.'"[6] Although the mottoes accompanying the scenes in the pattern book did not appear on the ware, both the motto and the painted scene nicely fit Jane's situation. "Scotch horses," as explained in *The Oxford Dictionary of Nursery Rhymes,* a variation of the late-eighteenth-century "Bell horses" nursery rhyme, were used to start races or

inaugurate festive occasions.[7] When this "rough colt" cracks the
bowl by tossing her paint box, the boys in the painting come alive,
introduce themselves to Jane and invite her into their world. The
child's sojourn "back in the Past," where she is promised to "be the
Spoilt One, the Darling, the Treasure" (75, 74), becomes increasingly ominous and imprisoning, until she is literally pulled away
by Mary Poppins and returned to feeling "safe and warm and
comforted" (78) at 17 Cherry Tree Lane. While rescuing the child,
Mary Poppins had lost her initialed, checked scarf which reap-
pears in Shepard's closing illustration for the chapter, as part of
the scene in the "Doulton" bowl—"as though someone had
dropped it as they ran" (88). Such a vestigial proof of the reality
of the dream is, of course, a well-tried literary device. Guillaume
de Machaut's *Le dit de la fonteinne amoureuse,* for instance,
which was a source for the Ceyx and Alcyone episode of Chaucer's
Book of the Duchess, features the dream of a disconsolate lover
during which his lady exchanges her ruby ring for his diamond
one. The lord awakens to find her ruby on his finger, an occur-
rence testified to by the poet-scribe himself. In the Mary Poppins
books, Jane and Michael are usually the reliable witnesses to
these transformations. It is this imprinting of what is accepted as
reality with an imaginative or mysterious feature, acknowledging
the links between past and present, the everyday and the fantastic, the seen and the unseen, that characterizes the heightened
reality of Mary Poppins, which no catalogue can fully capture or
describe.

Some features of this "cosmic nanny"[8] are very prominent. Her
quickness to diagnose, assess, and measure the behavior of the
Banks children, as she does in opening segments of the first three
books by administering medicine, thrusting a thermometer into
their mouths, and stretching a tape measure along their heights,
betokens a certain righteousness on her part. I am referring to
the "righteousness" (צֶדֶק :*sedek*) of the Old Testament (Deuteronomy 25.15; Leviticus 19.36; Ezekiel 45.10) which fills the measure and meets a standard. Her participation in the Hamadryad's
Grand Chain ("Full Moon," *MP*); the greeting she receives in the
constellations' golden ring, "a swaying . . . mass of horns and

hooves and manes and tails," which recalls Travers' "Zodiac
Circus" ("The Evening Out," *MPCB*); her recognition at the
Terrapin's party ("High Tide," *MPOD*); and her birthday-eve celebration with shadows ("Hallowe'en," *MPIP*) indicate that this
nanny surpasses all ordinary conventions and chronology. These
celebrations are, strictly speaking, liturgical, which makes all the
more sense when one traces the Hamadryad's observation, "that
to eat and be eaten are the same thing" (*MP* 172), to "The Hymn
of Christ" in the Apocryphal *Acts of John*. Before His crucifixion,
as the seer relates, Jesus gathered His brethren around Him and
chanted a catalogue of active and passive states, one verse of
which claims "'I will eat, / And I will be eaten.'"[9] Mary Poppins
seems to come from another world and time, and yet to be also a
futuristic model of understanding. Hers is a syncretistic belief in
unity, imagination, multeity, and wisdom, as a variety of like-
minded spokespersons attests. The Hamadryad insists that "bird
and beast and stone and star—we are all one, all one" (*MP* 173).
When the children query the Sun about the difference between
"what is real and what is not," his answer is a poetic one, "that to
think a thing is to make it true" (*MPCB* 182). The Terrapin reminds them of the sea's importance as originator and model of
their world: "the land came out of the sea . . . [and] each thing on
the earth has a brother here" (*MPOD* 170). The Bird Woman lets
them see the transporting value of the shadow, "the other part of
you, the outside of your inside," as a way to wisdom, which goes
"through things, through and out on the other side" (*MPIP* 212).

Mary Poppins and her bevy of acquaintances promote the celebration, harmony, and connectedness of all creation, which, according to the Hamadryad, is composed of "the same substance,
. . . all one, all moving to the same end" (*MP* 173). For the more
lyrical Mr. Twigley it consists of the "true music . . . [for] everything in the world—trees, rocks and stars and human beings"
(*MPOD* 41). Although Mary Poppins has phenomenal abilities,
such as ushering in Spring overnight, and exceptional friends
such as the Pleiades, she also exemplifies and extols trusted human virtues like loyalty and compassion. She offers her handker-
chief as a cushion for the sleeping Robertson Ay, and tells a story

("The Cat that Looked at a King," *MPOD*) in which the sagacious cat is not able to dissuade the queen, prime minister, and page from loyalty to their feckless king. Travers herself delights in stories with inclusivity as their theme. The romp "in the crack" between the old year and the new ("Happy Ever After," *MPOD*) and the Tramp–Angel's awareness of everyone's illusions ("Every Goose a Swan," *MPIP*) are moving instances of her storyteller's desire to embrace and possibly heal all. This urge is incarnated in the almost biblical figure of the Bird Woman, whose position "as a mother hen spread[ing] out her wings" (*MP* 110) summons up the divine protection described in Deuteronomy 32.11 and Matthew 23.37.

For all their emphasis on extraordinariness and attunement, the Mary Poppins books, at least the narrative structures of the first quartet, also raise some questions about this singular heroine. It is curious that this talented figure must pass through so many entrances and exits to the various episodes, as well as blow into and whirl out of the Banks family home three times. Is such narrative *to-ing* and *fro-ing* a reminder from Travers that this mythic creature, with a foot in reality, must also submit to the logical interrogatives of how, when, and where? Furthermore, Mary Poppins' very peremptory refusals to answer questions and her outright denials of involvement in fantastic events raise the issue of deliberately jeopardized credibility. Is this reverse psychology? Does Mary Poppins deny so vociferously, to incite readers to believe in, affirm, and acclaim her all the more enthusiastically? There are also some logical problems about Mary Poppins' vanity. Although never seen shopping for herself, collecting her pay, or spending her own earnings, she nevertheless takes great pride in her mysteriously acquired and uniformly prim clothes. Despite the discernment of her gimlet eyes, she proves amazingly susceptible to Michael's transparent flattery. Is this Poppins peccadillo meant to corroborate her essential childlikeness? The very fact that such questions can be asked underscores both Mary Poppins' complexity and Travers' art in sustaining the attraction and unpredictability of her heroine.

Among the more curious examples of her childhood reading, Travers has listed George Edward Farrow's *The Wallypug of Why* (1895). This admission might pique curiosity about possible residual influences of this odd, late Victorian fantasist on Travers' Mary Poppins books. Comparing Farrow's text with Travers' merely confirms the originality of her work. In contrast to the calm—albeit unnerving—omniscience of Mary Poppins and her subtly inculcated lessons about an interrelated and a potentially symphonic universe, Farrow's series of nonsensical misadventures are triggered by Carrollean word games (puns mainly). His frenzied diversion recreates the afternoon dream of the character "Girlie." In the topsy-turvy land of Why, where the powerless Wallypug is "governed by the people instead of governing them," Girlie searches for the meaning of the cryptic term "goo," found in a letter she had received that morning. Instead of answers, she is treated to a lecture "by A. Fish, Esq." on "'The Whichness of the What as compared to the Thatness of the Thus'"; whisked away to the Wallypug's "Fancy Dinner Party" (where "'you must fancy that you have got it'") with such delicacies as Air Soup, Half Soles and Heels (fried), Roast Grief, Snowball Fritters, High Jinks, Frolic Sauce and Mere Nothings on the menu ("'because it's what they *mean you* to have, and . . . because it's between *me and you*'"); and placed in a railway carriage with the demanding and cheeky letters of the alphabet as fellow passengers who interrogate her alliteratively.[10] The protracted linguistic games of this farrago, which do not resolve anything, come to an abrupt end: Girlie discovers the answer when, on being awakened for tea, she realizes that the troubling word is actually "good."

Since no sources or models for Travers' most famous character are to be found, the few extensive studies of her work attempt, instead, to explore its mythic and intertextual riches. Humphrey Carpenter's breezy assessment of the "disjointed air" of the books, in which "magic is used rather arbitrarily," does not tally with my own reading of their events, which can be discrete or interrelated, and their often-formulaic but never repeated scenarios; his observations, moreover, on Mary Poppins as "not a real English nanny

. . . but . . . an overstrained domestic servant"[11] fall far short of
the mark. Equally severe but limited is Perry Nodelman's claim
about her heartlessness, comparing Mary Poppins to Peter Pan
and Kenneth Grahame's Pan as "the least involving, the least lov-
able and least frightening of these Pan figures." More concerned
with justifying the exclusion of *Mary Poppins* from volumes devoted to "the best in children's literature," than with examining
the rich complexity of the figure herself, Nodelman rests his case
against the book on Travers' insistent focus on the heroine, as-
serting that the novel "reads . . . like a public relations release for
its star performer."[12] Similarly, Laura Hoffeld's simplistic demar-
cation of old and young, suggesting that in the books "adults
know less than children," and that the Banks as parents are "Dagwood Bumpsteads, well-meaning but hopelessly out of touch with
reality,"[13] is at odds with the facts. Mary Poppins' talented relatives and many of the Banks's neighbors are kindred spirits; Mr.
Banks himself appreciates the mystery of the stars and the plea-
sures of dancing, whisking his wife into an impromptu waltz on
one occasion. In *Mary Poppins and Myth,* Staffan Bergsten
ranges over a wide field of possible connections and parallels,
from the Bible, Virgil, Homer, the Chinese painter Wu Tao-tsz,
Dante, Blake, Wordsworth, Hoffman, and de la Mare to the less
likely Barrie, to substantiate his thesis that in Travers' quartet
"the normal relationship between art and life is turned inside
out."[14] Jonathan Cott's interview with Travers focuses on the ap-
preciative awareness of Blake, gnostic texts, and Zen philosophy
in her work, and records her admission, "Anything I write is all
question."[15] Fresh and positive commentary on Mary Poppins, a
portion of which prefaces *MPHND,* comes from a classicist spe-
cializing in Aristophanic comedy. With ardor and conviction, Kenneth J. Reckford claims that Travers has written "Dionysian"
fairy tales which allow "a wonderful transforming energy" to
break through "into ordinary life," but which also submit these
"Daemonic energies" to the control of Mary Poppins, "who is sur-
rounded by the magic and excitement that she helps generate,
but never really affected or altered by it."[16] He holds up the "hope-

fulness and joy" of these "transformations as criteria for examining Aristophanes' Dionysian comedies as fairy tales.

Disney's *Mary Poppins* (1963), for which Travers served as "Consultant," is a less effective guide or introduction to her work than Aristophanes' comedies. Although Travers had hoped, as she admitted in *Conversations*, "that its effect [would] be to bring more people to the books," she confesses to being "disturbed at seeing it so externalized, so oversimplified, so generalized."[17] Far from the subtlety, suggestiveness, and mythical allusions of the books, the film is designed to highlight the singing, dancing, and comedic skills of Julie Andrews, Dick Van Dyke, and an acrobatic ensemble, along with the talented animators employed by Disney Studios. More than a decade before the widespread use of special effects (that is, when Steven Spielberg and George Lucas were themselves just teenagers), this *Mary Poppins* features Bert, one of Van Dyke's two roles, dancing with animated penguins, and the heroine, as played by Julie Andrews with wired corsets, pink frilled crinolines, and cosmetic charm, bounding over a race course on an animated, wooden, merry-go-round horse. The Edwardian setting, which Travers apparently suggested to Disney, in order to retain the tale's "freshness," and the frothiness of Glynis Johns as Mrs. Banks in a trivializing Suffragette get-up, are not the most saddening or unfaithful aspects of this adaptation. What is most jarring, and what probably argues most persuasively against making such a book into a film, is the use of cartooned figures to translate and invariably reduce the fantasy. It was most instructive to see the film again, more than twenty-five years after its release, in a cinema crowded with youngsters and parents bent on reliving and sharing some of their own childhood. The animated segments did not grip the fidgety children, and even the well intentioned adults were yawning through this overlong exercise in slickness rather than art. I could not help thinking that these children were being cheated of the real thing. Nor could I resist noting some of the more problematic ironies: namely, the discrepancy between Travers' *New English Weekly* criticism of the saccharine travesty of Disney's animated "Snow

White" and her later involvement with this project, which per-
forms as great a disservice to the original; the addition of "numbers" about the importance of bank accounts, money making, and
steady employment, mundanities which seem totally removed
from the heightened reality of the books; and the decision to re-
make the slender, almost androgynous, figure of Mary Poppins
into a fussy, petticoat-flipping coquette of a musical comedy star.

The inevitable reduction of magic involved in such commercial-
ization did not pass unnoticed, even during the film's heyday in
the mid to late sixties. Peter and Dorothy Bart examined the
seven differently priced editions of "Mary Poppins" books, published by Whitman and Golden Books, both subsidiaries of West-
ern Publishing, a major outlet for Disney material. In addition to
the "aggressive mediocrity" of the style, and the obscuring of
Travers' own name in "minute type in the copyright footnote," the
Barts lamented the fact that "Walt Disney's Mary Poppins" essentially "mongrelized the classics."[18] Rosemary Smith also pointed
to the critical failure of the Golden Book version to understand
the meaning and mercurial essence of Mary Poppins' magic. In
making the nanny "less complex, . . . less obnoxious, . . . [and] less
delightful,"[19] the transformed story, in Smith's view, presented a
mere domestic employee and obliterated the need for her magic.

It seems certain that Mary Poppins attracts readers because of
her very complexity, her inexplicability. It is not simply that she
never explains, but that she herself cannot be dissected or re-
solved. Mary Shepard's line drawings present a tailored and trim,
poised and sensible woman; the dark hair scraped away from the
face and bound in a knot at the back of her head draws attention
to the all important expressivity of her eyes and voice. Travers'
friend and mentor, the poet AE, saw traces of ancient goddesses,
possibly the Indian Terrible Mother Kali, in this creature; as he
envisioned "Popkins," she "would undoubtedly have had long
golden tresses, a wreath of flowers in one hand, and perhaps a
spear in the other."[20] Feenie Ziner reports Travers' own disclosure
of a remark made by a Zen priest that Mary Poppins is "full of
Zen," since "in every Zen story there is always a single object
which contains a secret."[21] Jonathan Cott pursues connections be-

tween Mary Poppins and the "Ecstatic Mother," as exemplified in
Artemis and Sophia.[22] It is beneficial to allow all these possibilities to coexist, since each reader discerns in this nanny one salient characteristic which itself reflects on the idiosyncracies of the
reader. Mary Poppins preserves a certain innocence (*not* näiveté)
and joyous trust. Although not overtly religious or sermonizing,
her influence, at once purposive and universal, is encoded in the
acronyms with which Travers closes each book: either A.M.G.D.
(*ad majorem gloriam Dei:* to the greater glory of God), which is,
incidentally, the motto of the Jesuits, or G.I.E.D. (*gloria in excel-
sis Deo:* glory to God in the highest). As sympathetically attuned
to the baby Annabel's preverbal utterances as she is protective of
the eccentricity of her relatives and friends, Mary Poppins is a
rendition of the Pauline fool. With inversions reminiscent of
Paul's slippery irony in making the wisdom of God the folly of men
(I Corinthians 1.18–27), Mary Poppins plunges into episodes,
which might seem mere magical escapades to some, but which
remain cheering, promise-filled realities to the wise.

6

The Mary Poppins Books:
Everything Inside Something Else

> "There's always a cloud about somewhere," said
> Mary Poppins, comfortably. And she set a match to
> the wick of the nightlight where it stood on the man-
> telpiece, a small and glowing likeness of the big
> lamp on the table. As usual, it would watch all night.
> And the two lamps filled the room with shadows
> that were themselves like clouds.
> —*Mary Poppins and the House Next Door,* 1988

The pensive, Platonically-inspired Jane Banks muses at one point on the connectedness of all things, wondering if her park of plasticene blobs could actually be the model or prototype for a bigger, enveloping construct. Her "little park inside the big one and the big one inside a larger one? Again and again? Away and away?" (*MPIP* 187). This nesting box effect is one way to view the relationship of the books in the Poppins canon, and especially that of the sextet (*MP, MPCB, MPOD, MPIP, MPCTL, MPHND*) itself. These books share such features as energetic transformations; reconciled opposites; and heightened awareness of reality through dream, through the other, and through memory of the past. There also appears to be a distinct and developing sense of narrative art, linking the episodes of the first four books with the stories of the last two. As the series proceeds, the individuation of the Banks children is more precise, and the psychological realism of their characters more detailed. In addition, as the references to books themselves increase, in *MPOD* and *MPIP*, Travers' own fabulation becomes more noticeably self-conscious. Her return to the Poppins vein over a quarter of a century later in *MPCTL* and *MPHND,* or, as she would prefer to put it, the surprising return visit of Mary Poppins to her consciousness, shows a desire to re-examine the same issues, without episodic fragmentation but by blending all the old themes into discrete, full length stories.

Although it would be misguided to fix on *MP* as the sole criterion for judging the series, this first book does, in many ways, set the tone for all that follows. It introduces several dualities: a world of experiences anchored in, yet transcending, domestic reality; a heroine characterized by nannylike common sense, but gifted with mesmerizing capabilities; and a host of ordinary and extraordinary circumstances, which invest Mary Poppins, the inverter of expectations, with an aura of awe and mystery.

The search by the reader, the "you" addressed in the first sentence, for Cherry Tree Lane begins with mythic appropriateness "at the cross-roads" (*MP* 1). The decision to proceed seems eminently sensible, according to the sharp particulars of the policeman's directions. In fact, however, going to Cherry Tree Lane involves stepping over a threshold, away from the carefully plotted realm of left and right turns, and into a world where domestic reality and pastoral dream run parallel. Yet, in contravention of geometric principles, these two realities periodically meet, thanks to the interlacing motif of dance. Travers' initial, wide angle description of the place, "where the houses run down one side and the Park runs down the other and the cherry-trees go dancing right down the middle" (*MP* 1), ushers the reader into this curious, hybrid cosmos. Quite deliberately she takes the reader by the hand, fashioning the conditional clauses which begin the first three paragraphs—"if you want to find Cherry-Tree Lane," "if you follow his direction," and "if you are looking for Number 17"—into a logical progression and thus building confidence in a narrator, who seems to have the reader's interest and enjoyment at heart.

Another way in which Travers mollifies any resistance to the singularity surrounding Mary Poppins is by describing the already sufficiently fanciful experiences in Cherry Tree Lane. The Banks themselves are likable embodiments of exaggerated practicality; Mr. Banks, who had offered his wife the option of having "either a nice, clean, comfortable house or four children" (*MP* 1), dons two overcoats to meet the blast of the east wind. In a confiding, chatty tone, Travers throws into the gently simmering narrative pot apparently inconsequential details about a neighboring house "built exactly like a ship" (*MP* 3), and a glimpse of the latest nanny, Katie Nanna, who "was old and fat and smelt of barley water" (*MP* 5). Even though Mary Poppins, initially mistaken for the returning Mr. Banks, arrives on a gust of east wind which shakes the whole house and causes Michael to remark that he had "never seen that happen before" (*MP* 6), Travers quickly establishes the heroine's uniqueness in relation to the Cherry Tree Lane norm. This new applicant, who is "thin with large feet and hands, and small, rather peering blue eyes" (*MP* 6), turns the tables on Mrs. Banks by refusing to give references, and creating the impression that she is actually assessing the eligibility of the Banks to obtain her services. The children are awestruck by her matter of fact magic: sliding up the banisters, producing her strictly useful possessions from an empty carpet bag, dispensing surprisingly sweet and variously flavored medicines from a single bottle, and preparing them for bed with lightning speed. Rather than making Jane and Michael nervous, her terse responses intrigue them; the more impulsive and demonstrative Michael even begs Mary Poppins, on her first night in their nursery, never to leave them. The bond between her and the children is cemented as much by her brusqueness, as by her firm yet sympathetic adult presence. Neither bored with her charges, nor infantilized by their demands, Mary Poppins is clearly at home in the nursery, and entirely capable of dealing with their curious questions. With nunlike fastidiousness, she undresses beneath the tent of her nightgown and, rather than cajoling Michael, she short-circuits his attempt to extract a promise by agreeing to stay "till the wind changes" (*MP* 14) at the same time as, generating her own wind, she blows out her candle.

Mary Poppins is, among other things, a woman of her word. After blowing in on the east wind, and participating in ten distinct adventures, she departs, as promised, when the wind changes, carried aloft at the end of her umbrella by a west wind. Between coming and going—with a promise of return nestled in the *au revoir* note—Mary Poppins has stepped into the action of a chalk picture on the sidewalk; presided at a levitated afternoon tea; reunited a pampered pet with its fretful owner; regaled Jane with a story of a dancing cow in search of a fallen star; travelled to the points of the compass with Michael until his anger melts; taken the children to visit with the Bird Woman of St. Paul's; introduced them to Mrs. Corry's candy and gingerbread shop; discoursed on the way of the world to the infant twins, Barbara and John; led the Grand Chain in the "Full Moon" celebration at the zoo; and assisted the star Maia in her unconventional Christmas shopping. Similarly, the eight adventures of *MPCB* are sandwiched between her reentry on a kite string and her whirling out again on a merry-go-round, that rises into the sky. Her request of a "return" ticket for the merry-go-round keeps alive the children's hopes for her return, which, despite the delay of eight years, relies on the now standard entry and exit frames. In *MPOD,* she swirls into the story as part of the Guy Fawkes' Day fireworks display, and after six adventures, she passes through a door, leaving the children once more.

Although the children's ages and the family's circumstances remain unchanged in this third book, certain shifts in narrative style and thematic preoccupations signal Travers' more self-conscious concern for storytelling. In the face of the children's sorrow at Mary Poppins' departure, the narrator clarifies the cosmic importance of this heroine as a force embedded in nature and the seasons: "The rain and the sun would remind them of her, and the birds and the beasts and the changing seasons" (*MPOD* 235). In addition to such clues about her permanence, the number of literary allusions increases in this book, too. Earlier, when Mary

Poppins' description of her adventure in the chalk picture as a "Fairyland" had evoked questions from the children about possible encounters with Cinderella and Robinson Crusoe, she had sniffed pityingly at their inquiries with the idiosyncratic (though grammatically incorrect) explanation, that "'everybody's got a Fairyland of their own'" (*MP* 28). Now references to books—nursery classics along with childhood ephemera—are taken much more seriously in *MPOD*. The episode with the talking statue begins with the curiosity of the Marble Boy, Neleus, about the conclusion of one of Kipling's *Just So Stories*. As Neleus explains to the gentleman over whose shoulder he had been reading, "'I wanted to finish the Elephant story and see how he got his trunk'" (*MPOD* 94). Neleus's friendship with Jane and Michael is secured through his allusions to books; he testifies about knowing *Alice in Wonderland* "by heart," "most of *Robinson Crusoe*," *Everything a Lady Should Know* (which he accurately labels "Mary Poppins' favourite"), and the adventures of Tiger Tim in the *Lot-o'-Fun* comics (*MPOD* 100). Books are more than nursery fixtures in the "Happy Ever After" chapter: Mary Poppins positions "three well-known books: *Robinson Crusoe, The Green Fairy Book* and *Mother Goose Nursery Rhymes*" (178, in front of the stuffed animals, alerting Jane to the fact that something is about to happen; and "in the crack" between the old year and the new, toys and book characters dance and cavort together. Another feature which indicates the heightened artistic consciousness of this book, and paves the way for its sequel is the ending, which deals with reflection, mirroring, and the Platonic realm of models and replicas. Previously, Mary Poppins had been carried aloft by an umbrella or on the back of a merry-go-round horse, but now she steps through a reflected door into "field on field of sky, and the dark spreading night" (231). Shimmeringly located in the nursery, this exit alludes to aspects of the other farewells. Mary Poppins glances back swiftly "towards the Nursery" (231), snaps open the umbrella, and clears the tree tops to the peal of the hurdygurdy's music. It is without doubt the most resonant and complex of the endings. The nursery is a world of experiences, a reflection of things past, and an intimation of those to come. The effect of

Mary Poppins, with her identifying, parrot headed umbrella and constant associations with music and dance, is meant to be long-lasting, not just while Mr. and Mrs. Banks waltz around the nursery to the hurdy-gurdy's tune, but forever as attested by the children's skyward declaration, "'we'll never forget you, Mary Poppins!'" (235).

None of the remaining books is concerned with her comings and goings. However, they continue to draw on her hallmark features and remarkable transforming capabilities. Because *MPIP* is a collection of six separate escapades, which occurred some time during her three visits, it should be considered in connection with the three earlier books. Moreover, in *MPIP,* Travers continues the literariness emergent in *MPOD,* at the same time as she polishes each individual story as the vehicle of a particular lesson or insight. Often she uses fairy tale motifs: Michael's adventures on the Cat Star, in the "Lucky Thursday" chapter, turn on his success or failure in answering three riddles. Stories in books, as opposed, say, to chalk sketches on the pavement, are more prominent as the motives and sources of escapades in *MPIP;* and the traditional storybooks themselves, as in "The Children in the Story," convey a family tradition and a sense of timelessness, merely through offering evidence, in their worn and faded shape, of the generations of little hands which have held them. In turning the pages of *The Silver Fairy Book,* Jane realizes that "it had belonged to Mrs. Banks, and before that it had been given to her mother by *her* mother" (*MPIP* 112). The pictures also tell a tale, since "many . . . had disappeared and the drawings had all been coloured with crayons, either by Jane and Michael or by their mother. Perhaps, even, by their Grandmother, too" (112). The three princes brought to life in the story, who strike up a conversation with Jane and Michael, attempt to dissuade the children from separating "Once Upon a Time" from the here and now; as Prince Veritain protests, "'it's always'" (115). The closing Halloween celebrations of shadows in the park strengthen his point. When Jane doubts that Cock Robin could possibly be a part of the festivities, since "'he's a Nursery Rhyme,'" the "phantom bird," corrects her: "'you can't have a shadow without a substance—

anyone knows that!'" (207). Significantly the "reeling, romping dance" unites fairy tale and nursery rhyme characters, along with the kindred spirits and relatives of Mary Poppins' earlier escapades (214).

In a broader sense, the desire to unite wish with reality, the inside with the outside, and the past with the present, underlies the themes of each of this book's six stories. The Bird Woman's final pithy comment, that "'seeking's finding'" (225), suitably closes a collection that starts with Mary Poppins' charge against Michael, Jane, and the Park Keeper: "'always wanting to be something else instead of what you are'" (6). Although some conclusions, such as Mary Poppins' pronouncement that "Faithful Friends should be together, never apart" (65) and the Lord Chamberlain's declaration in the kingdom of the Cat Star, that "all wishes are important" (86), may sound a little prosaic, the crucial notion reverberating throughout this collection is the importance of memory as a means of integrating childhood and adulthood. The willingness of Florimond, Veritain, and Amor to step out of their story, gently encourages Miss Lark, the Professor, and the Park Keeper to remember who they have been, as well as who they are. Though only a plasticene figure, Mr. Mo offers sound advice to Jane, who is distressed at having to leave behind her exquisitely created little park. In Mr. Mo's counsel, "'as long as you remember it, you can always come and go'" (181). Jane's resulting determination "never to forget" captures the essence of the whole quartet of Mary Poppins books. The child's optimism about tracing a way back to her park—"somehow, somewhere, . . . she knew she would find it again—as neat and as gay and as happy as it had been today" (190–91)—is reminiscent of the boy–narrator's enthusiasm about relocating his Happy Isle in Kenneth Grahame's "Its Walls Were As of Jasper." Jane's eagerness to search, and her resolution to remember, express the heritage bequeathed by Mary Poppins.

The most recent works, *MPCTL* and *MPHND,* are major additions to the Poppins canon. They stretch back to the earliest books and attempt to incorporate two lonely outsiders, the Park Keeper and Miss Andrew, into a world where past and present, earth and sky, and all points in between connect. Since harmonious inclusion has been one of Travers' most favored themes, it makes sense that she would turn so sympathetically, and beckoningly, to these two easily ridiculed, and often dismissed characters. Moreover, since what gerontologists call "life reviews" are probably prominent in Travers' own thoughts, it is only appropriate that the loyal Poppins readers be given an opportunity to sift through and try to make sense of the lives of these two isolates.

MPCTL really concerns the uses of enchantment. Set in the park during a supper picnic on Midsummer's Eve—a bewitching time when one can meet one's true love, enter another world, and experience a different time—the story pays particular attention to the effects of "the moonstruck moment, the trance, the dream, whatever it was"[1] on Frederick Smith, the Park Keeper. Although poor Smith does not understand the importance of this liminal time which, like the moments "in the crack" of *Happy Ever After,* exists in the interval, "not day, not night, but something between—the hour that is thronged with fate" (29), he longs to be part of some pattern of completeness.

> The world went strolling past in pairs, two by two, hand in hand. Would such a thing ever happen to him? ...
> Would anyone—Snow White, say, or Cinderella—hide her face in *his* serge jacket? (29)

In giving "himself to the twilight," he closes his eyes and walks backward to the past, where "distant music" and "old songs he seemed to have known as a boy" (30), waft toward him. But not finding "the longed-for 'she'" (34), and seeing his world of "lawful authority" (43) and orderly conduct dissolve, when Orion, Castor and Pollux, and other constellations descend to join the celebrations in the park, the Park Keeper feels perplexed and, once again, left out. For a man to whom these celestials are "'characters in a story'" (39), or "'just a bunch of stars'" (41), and who indignantly insists that he is "'not somebody else'" (45), some sobering advice about his identity and social responsibility are in order. And who better to deliver these observations than the chief of the descending celestials, Orion? Tagged with the wonderful understatement of "the big man," this gigantic hunter was, according to Homer (*Odyssey* 11. 309–10), bigger and more handsome than the Aloadae, Otus and Ephialtes, who grew to be nine fathoms tall and nine cubits broad, when they were only nine years old. Swathed in a lion skin and bright as the sun, Orion informs the Park Keeper, with matter-of-fact directness, that "'everyone's somebody else to someone'" (45). Through his participation in the Grand Chain in the herb garden, to the tune of the nightingale's song and the toy top's hum, this luminous being leads Smith to a moment of insight: "like a man who has lost, and regained, his senses, the Park Keeper understood" (60). Seeing "the familiar solid and substantial shapes of Mary Poppins and her charges, Mrs. Corry and her two large daughters, his Mother in her shabby shawl," dancing with "the bevy of transparent figures, the creatures that seemed to be made of light" (60), prompts him to remember and renew the trust he had "when he was a boy" (60). On a larger scale, this reunification of past and present, which affects Mr. Banks as well, parallels the story's overarching connections between earth and sky, known and unknown worlds. Returning from their picnic, the children see the link joining well known houses to far off galaxies. "It se emed as though each house in the Lane, leaning so closely to the next, had lit itself from its neighbour. There were constellations both below and above, the earth and the sky were next door to each other" (81). Furthermore, true to the form of all Mary Poppins' episodes, there is proof of the reality of the fantastic transformation. When *fossicking* (an Australian term for "hunting" or "searching") among the curly fronds, Lepus finds a shiny half-crown piece, which Orion places in his belt; and one of the departing creatures, possibly Philomel, gives Mary Poppins a glowing wing feather, with which she decorates her hat. Although Mr. Banks is ecstatic at what he assumes to be a new star, the children are aware of the origin of this extra brightness, and its relationship to Mary Poppins' resplendent hat. "Their adventure had, indeed, been true. At last they could believe it. And, meeting Mary Poppins' eyes, they knew that she knew what they knew. All things, indeed, were possible—sky-light upon an earthy hat-brim, earth-light on a skyey girdle" (85).

There are more venues for action in *MPHND;* but Travers' emphasis on incorporation and harmony remains undiminished, making Humphrey Carpenter's dismissive comment on the book as "a lightweight encore"[2] seem uninformed and misguided. When Miss Andrew, Mr. Banks's old nanny, takes over the deserted house at 18 Cherry Tree Lane, the wheels of this latest escapade are set in motion. Since her memorable appearance in *MPCB*, the ferocious, opinionated Miss Andrew has been associated with the idea of imprisonment. On that occasion she kept a lark in a cage; in this book she so dictatorially monopolizes the time of Luti, the houseboy she has brought back from the South Seas, that he is effectively caged. The only other glimpse readers have had of Miss Andrew is her ignominious predicament at the end of the Anglerfish's line at the High Tide party *(MPOD),* a position which even the sensitive Jane considered most appropriate. Travers is now definitely trying to reclaim and humanize Miss Andrew through a story, in which the cloud-hopping return of Luti to the South Seas, close to Travers' own native Australia, parallels the attempted integration of Miss Andrew into a society of mutual respect and responsibilities. The meeting of Mary Poppins, the children, and Luti with the Man in the Moon is the pivotal episode, not only for sending Luti back to his family, but for bringing Miss Andrew into a community, too. Hailed as Mary Poppins' "uncle"—which makes him one of many—the Man in the Moon binds together all aspects of the tale. He is first seen about to drink cocoa, made from a tin of cocoa which Jane had earlier dropped, and from a cup, which Mrs. Brill had broken at the outset of the story. He maintains "a kind of storehouse" for all lost things, and knows everyone; it is his job "to watch and wake."[3] This makes his awareness of the hardships suffered by Luti's family, and his return of the lost, but unmusical, mouth organ to Michael entirely plausible. Mary Poppins as the phenomenal agent of reunification, fashions a sarong of her shawl for Luti, and gives the boy directions for getting home, "pointing to a string of cloudlets that floated like puffballs in the blue" (66). She also proves to be the only one who can play the mouth organ, with a tune that causes even the "stone figure" (78) of Miss Andrew to join in the hornpipe. Reluctant though it is, Miss Andrew's dancing is the signal of her movement toward others. Luti's consistent goodness is echoed in the benediction with which he enters and leaves the scene: "'Peace and Blessings!'" (66). Miss Andrew's transformation, from deserted harridan to a member of Admiral Boom's household (who reads *Fizzo* comics to the pirate Binnacle) is not without pain or problems. She blames Mary Poppins for bamboozling her, causing her to "perform [in] so shameful, so undignified" a manner (80). Yet the dance connects Miss Andrew to the motif of joy and association central to the books—from Mrs. Corry's Highland fling (*MP* 123), Maia's twinkling step (*MP* 186), Mary Poppins' waltz with the Sun (*MPCB* 182) and hornpipe (*MPOD* 168), Jane and Michael's twirling (*MPOD* 41), and even to the Park Keeper's Highland fling (*MPIP* 222)—and precedes her welcome into the Boom home where, in the Admiral's words, "'she's safely in port, . . . on an even keel'" (81).

Critical comments on Travers' accomplishment, especially in the first four books, have not stayed at such an even keel. In an early review, Anne Carroll Moore welcomed the first book as "a Pleasure of the first water," managing to be both "fantastic, without whimsy or sweetness, and human without dwelling on the obvious."[4] While John Rowe Townsend wonders if the American popularity of the books might not propagate "illusions about English domestic life," Jane Yolen lionizes Travers as a maker of or, more accurately, believer in myth, who presents "strong, beautiful, alternate worlds for young people."[5] Neither Albert V. Schwartz nor Robert B. Moore, however, is convinced of the strength and beauty of the world presented in the "Bad Tuesday" chapter of *MP*. Schwartz charges that it is "a racist nightmare," teaching "children to identify their fears with Third World people."[6] Moore, Director of the Racism/Sexism Resource Center for Education in New York City, refuses to accept the innocence of the stereotypes of the Eskimo, Black, Chinese and Indian, all weapon wielding, "threatening and full of revenge" (*MP* 100). In view of his desire "to promote children's literature free of race, sex, class, handicap, or age bias," and to recognize "the impact of social conditioning," Moore ponders the effect of the book "on a child's self-image, personality, and image of others."[7] Although no changes were made when the copyright was renewed in 1962, Travers first revised the "Bad Tuesday" chapter for the 1972 paperback reissue by altering most of the "picaninny" language to standard English or, as she described it to Albert Schwartz: "Formal English, grave and formal." In the tense interview with Schwartz, Travers sounds more defensive and intransigent with each statement. "I refuse to be arraigned for what I wrote," she declared. "You're overstressing from the point of view of racism, which is something I don't accept." She insisted that *Mary Poppins* is "not a contemporary book" but a "timeless" one, derived from the imagination which is "a pure thing, . . . envisaging," and not dependent "upon the sociology of the time."[8] She did concede in this interview, however, that the book was written "a long time ago when racism was not as important," and that the altered conversations were her idea, prompted by the discomfort of "a schoolteacher friend," who shuddered and squirmed at reading the "Bad Tuesday" chapter, "if she had Black children in her class."[9] Travers has issued a substantially altered chapter in the Revised Version of *MP* (1981), which replaces the racial stereotypes with Polar Bear, Macaw, Dolphin and Panda. This Revised Version, part of Harcourt Brace Jovanovich's Voyager Book series of Mary Poppins stories, is now the only one for sale in most bookstores. Travers' explanation, in the pages of *Children's Literature,* puts the offending episode in the context of a chapter about the boy's sulky behavior.

> Michael—how unwisely!—had taken Mary Poppins' compass and used it without permission. Was it any wonder, then—wasn't it, even, inevitable?—that those from North, South, East and West would come to avenge their friend? It would seem a pity to defraud children of the idea—not deliberately put there by me but arising naturally from the story—of the difference between day and night, cause and effect, the contentment that comes when danger is past, the goodness of the bad![10]

Although she calls the revision "a gesture of gratitude, wry but valid, to the valiant protestors" (217), she is especially happy, in having reread the book, at discovering and correcting "an ethical mistake" (involving a single word) that had gone undetected. Rather than trying to force humor or relying on the plea of injured innocence, Travers might simply have recognized the differences in cultural expectations, and the influences of various struggles for equality over a period of almost half a century, which cannot be waved off as the mere sociology of the time. In the 1934 text, the "piccaninny" language of "the negro lady" inviting Mary Poppins to "'bring dem chillum dere into ma li'l house for a slice of water-melon right now'", and Michael's angry determination "not to be outrun by an Indian boy"[11] do hint at an unacceptable, however unwittingly embedded, racist bias. Travers' protest that "sometimes we do too much" to shelter and cosset children is sensible enough. No reader wants, or would enjoy, a totally sanitized literature. That would mean welcoming something as banal as the bowdlerized versions of nursery rhymes proposed by Barry Perlmutter in his *No More Nightmares: A Gentler Mother Goose*.[12] Critics are not asking that Mary Poppins be gentler, but that her fantastic peregrinations be genuinely liberating experiences, empowering young readers to live justly, openly, and harmoniously.

7

The Continuing Relevance of Myth and Fairy Tale: Summoned, Not Invented

> I am glad, therefore, to have kept my terror whole and thus retained a strong link with the child's things-as-they-are, where all things relate to one another and all are congruous.
>
> —*About the Sleeping Beauty*, 1975

In articulating her life long views about myth and fairy tale, Travers' most recent writing serves as a checklist for the articles of her creed. The essays, stories, retellings, and occasional poetry she published over the last three decades, and the interviews she has given, reiterate ideas and link her earliest memories and writing to her latest work. Zealously and repeatedly, she mentions the need to remain open, even vulnerable, to the myths and stories, whose tensions suffuse our lives. Glimpses of her childhood, snatches of her poetry and illuminating remarks on Mary Poppins, all tessellate the writing she is undertaking in her seventies and eighties. The past is not blocked out; on the contrary, it remains a wellspring of wonder and sorrow, a reason for trust and reconciliation, and a platform for launching tentative speculations about the whole of her life.

Travers' long brooding on the monkey lord Hanuman, of Hindu myth, has resulted in the full length story, *Friend Monkey* (1971). During her interview with Jonathan Cott, she conceded that she would like "so much" to see the book made into a film, "but certainly not as a cartoon, for you must show the sorrow and the grief and the endless love that is in Monkey."[1] She praises Monkey as the exemplification of all three types of love—chemical, emotional, and spiritual—and bases her assessment on the belief that "too much is better than too little" (231). At the time of its publication critics found the book altogether too much. The reviewer in the *New York Times Book Review* (7 November 1971) cites not only the "tiresome" stock characters but the overdone writing, full of "would-be poetic" adjectives and "strained" metaphors. Paul Heins' *Horn Book* review (February 1972) is not much more flattering. "A plethora of characters . . . of the flat comic variety," and a plot "boiling over" with incidents that are "ludicrous without being funny," hardly compensate for the lack of Mary Poppins' "wonderful deadpan magic."[2] Whether the current paperback reissue of the book (by Puffin in 1985, by Dell in 1987) suggests a renewed appreciation, remains to be seen. The difficulty with the earlier reviews is that they expect, and want, another Mary Poppins. That Travers has not supplied discrete episodes with fantastic romps and all important returns to the everyday, that she moves back in time from the Banks's life of the thirties to the London of the Diamond Jubilee (1897), and that she makes the eccentricity of her characters both periodic and endemic to the particular section of Putney where they live constitute some of the difficulties readers might face. But with a hero who does nothing by halves, *Friend Monkey* has an appropriately excessive style, one suited to the totality and completeness of its interrelated themes—of release from conventions and old moorings, and homecoming—however nonVictorian or utopian these may seem.

Travers has often commented on the figures who move the story along: Monkey; the Linnets, with whom Monkey comes to stay in Putney; Miss Brown-Potter, a retired explorer who lives next door; and Professor McWhirter, the kilt-clad, animal "fancier," bent on procuring Monkey for a zoo. In a later *Parabola* essay, "Re-storying the Adult" (8.4.1983, 51–53),[3] she lovingly relates Hanuman's exploits in the *Ramayana,* serving Rama and reuniting him with his beloved Sita, the "sole of his kind" who seeks "nothing for himself" (52). With "mind, heart, and body steadied on the task," Hanuman's "passion is to serve" (52–53). Travers also justifies her appropriation of this helper by claiming that the Hanuman figure could never disappear but simply move "from one cycle of stories to another" (53). In her adaptation, or extension, Monkey wreaks havoc on board ship, in the Linnets' home which actually belongs to the crochety Uncle Trehunsey, and at Miss Brown-Potter's, where they all move after the fire. The fascinatingly eccentric Miss Brown-Potter impresses Paul Heins as but "a faint reflection of Mary Poppins grown benign and philosophical." But Travers has revealed to Jonathan Cott a series of influences for the character, from Mary Kingsley, "the niece of Charles Kingsley, who went to West Africa and explored it," and "a family of Brown-Potters"[4] next to whom she lived as a child, to the childhood trials endured by Beatrix Potter (whose biography by Margaret Lane Travers reviewed in the *New English Weekly*). The plain, only child of handsome parents, Miss Brown-Potter is a captivating character. Her childhood experiences in the nursery, "isolated in her treetop world,"[5] correspond vaguely to the loneliness felt by Beatrix Potter. Travers has lavished great care on the animated memories and sounds that for this spinster still live in the house of her childhood, which she now shares with a deaf African orphan costumed as a Regency page. There is a vividness in Miss Brown-Potter's party memories which recalls the anecdotes of Aunt Sass. In fact, Travers' own recalled feelings, and her reminiscences of Aunt Sass's peculiarities may well have influenced her characterization of Miss Brown-Potter. Remembering the parties "with the swish of taffeta on the stairs, . . . the tinkle of silver on glass or china," and her own gawkish appearance as "a shy child in a long white dress," Miss Brown-Potter recollects and still hears the music of her past: "a clarinet piping an old tune, somebody playing the drawing-room piano, somebody else standing beside it, singing a song or a ballad" (96). Miss Brown-Potter names her pet badger and dog "Tinker" and "Badger," respectively. Aunt Sass "kept a succession of small dogs, two by two, and the pairs were always called Tinker and Badger, inheriting the names as though they were titles" (*Aunt Sass,* 15). Miss Brown-Potter's nomenclature relies on a similar and, to her, eminently sensible precedent. "'Well, my great-grandmother,' said Miss Brown-Potter, 'and for all I know, *her* great-grandmother, always had pets called Badger and Tinker. So had my grandmother, so had my mother, and so, of course, have I'" (101). However, for all these similarities, there seem to be as many differences separating Miss Brown-Potter from Beatrix Potter, Mary Poppins, and Aunt Sass. No bitterness corrodes Miss Brown-Potter's childhood memories; her parents live on as elegant revenants. Though single-minded and venturesome, Miss Brown-Potter shows none of Mary Poppins' censoriousness or Aunt Sass's belligerence. Calmly and determinedly she defuses Uncle Trehunsey's anger and a fluttery neighbour's complaints. Of the three central characters, though, the most problematic remains Professor McWhirter. The difficulty lies not with his cloying brogue, nor with his unpredictable appearances, but with his apparently menacing motives towards Monkey. Only when the Linnet and Brown-Potter households have boarded a cargo ship, to move to the remote African village of Umtota, is McWhirter's true identity as an animal "protector" revealed. Travers herself has admitted to Jonathan Cott that this upshot came "as a shock" to her too: "I didn't realize that Professor McWhirter wasn't a bad guy until that very end, I had no idea!"[6] The acceptance or rejection of McWhirter's role as a last minute rescuer is the critical decision to be made about *Friend Monkey*. If this disclosure impresses the reader as too abrupt, then the whole fanciful scheme to get to Umtota appears a desperate escape, not just from an intolerable situation in Putney, but from an overcomplicated and out of control plot. If, however, McWhirter's true role as *deus ex machina* is a credible surprise, then it fits ideally into the mercurial plot line, which so resembles a fairy tale. It will also be considered feasible that the two characters most open to Monkey's love, Mr. Linnet and Miss Brown-Potter, should lead the exodus which brings their families not to Umtota (which sounds both too stammering and totalizing) but to an unnamed, uncharted, and secret island where all their needs are met. The namelessness and isolation of this final locale are no drawbacks. The island's use as one of McWhirter's animal refuges both clarifies and ensures the need for continuing openness on the part of these new guardians. That the island also reunites Monkey with a simian clan, who honor him as their king, makes the locale the perfect home.

Travers' heroes wear many faces and travel widely. Monkey's peregrinations, along with his more illuminating than bungling helpfulness, are some indications of the multifacetedness of the hero and the omnipresence of myth, both absorbing topics for Travers. The ways in which myth can nourish fairy tale, as evidenced in *Friend Monkey,* also preoccupy her. She has pinned up her colors in many essays and talks. As an ever inquiring and lifelong devotee, she distinguishes the reverential serendipity of her approach from that of folklorists, anthropologists, and psychoanalysts. In "Only Connect," she sees fairy tales as "miniscule reaffirmations of myth . . . fallen into time and locality." Her Clark Lecture, at Scripps College in Claremont, California, "In Search of the Hero," reiterates her position, maintaining that "we live in myth and fairy tale as the egg yolk lives in its albumen" and that the hero, in each form, seeks to discover his or her self-identity. In the afterword to her retelling of Sleeping Beauty, Travers hints at many of the conditions—of narrative and attitude—which make this discovery possible. An "undifferentiated" world, without separation between self and milieu, is crucial to the fairy tale, and "common to all children" (47). The infinitude of this world, when "the time is always now and endless" (49), when nothing is explained, and when narrated events make their own links in our lives, is appropriate to her oft repeated axiom that thinking is linking, which she defines as "the essence of fairy tale" (50). The necessary catalyst of the tale, peril or the sense of being in jeopardy, leads to her disquisition on another favorite theme, the importance of the Wise Woman or Thirteenth Fairy. Comparing this figure to the Hindu goddess Kali, "who carries in her multiple hands the powers of good and evil" (56), Travers elevates her, "not the heroine, [as] the goddess in the machine" (57). In her retelling, Travers inserts an authorial aside about the need to thank the Thirteenth Wise Woman who, in calling forth the receiving power, illustrates the gnomic statement that "light is light because of the dark" (43).

The desire to explore such complex yet timeless ideas on the fairy tale, no doubt, lies behind *About the Sleeping Beauty* (1975). Its critical reception has been neither especially warm nor sympathetic; indeed, at times the reviews seem downright hostile. The *Kirkus Review* complained about the afterword as "repetitious and windy, . . . buried in self-infatuated blah."[7] Even as stalwart an admirer as Jonathan Cott, while grateful that Travers "has not forgotten that the fairy tale is the primer of the picture language of the soul," complains about the clumsiness and "flummery" of the retelling.[8] Michael Patrick Hearn finds the Arabian setting an unjustified "theatrical trick—a device similar to performing Shakespeare in modern dress or Bizet in blackface," and judges the "high intentions and dismal excesses" as capable of putting "a princess to sleep without aid of a spindle."[9] Although Joseph Cary admits that Travers' retelling is itself a "flawed" but "light-giving" diamond, he is most expansive in praising the "superb personal essay-meditation of the afterword."[10] Both Hearn and Cary, however, take exception to Charles Keeping's illustrations, which Hearn sees as "stiff" and "unremarkable," and Cary charges "emanate from the plastic world of Barbie and Ken."[11]

Travers defends her story's "vaguely Middle-Eastern world" as a deliberate attempt to get rid of "its attic clutter . . . in order to see its meaning clear."[12] Some images and descriptive passages, it is true, work extremely well. The picture of life stilled around the sleeping princess is caught adroitly in this simile: "the lizard lay still, like a scribble on marble" (25). Too often, though, Travers overloads passages, forcing this fairy tale to lecture on its own importance. As the hundred years pass, the story of the princess becomes, for the local folk, a fairy tale, "something forever true but far" (29). Not content with this label, Travers waxes in a Jungian mode. "Men came to think of the Princess, not as a person anymore, but as a secret within themselves—a thing they would dearly wish to discover if they could but make the effort" (29). The motif of self discovery is pronounced in this retelling, to the point of being cumbersomely underlined. As the prince gazes on the princess for the first time, Travers observes, "He knew himself to be at the centre of the world and that, in him, all men stood there, gazing at their hearts' desire—or perhaps their inmost selves" (36). Their kiss, which causes such cosmic reverberations, results in another series of over-dramatic events, as "together they plumbed all height, all depth, and rose up strongly to the surface, back to the shores of time" (37).

Her essays, anecdotes, retellings, and occasional poetry in *Parabola,* reiterate many similar arguments about myth and fairy tale. They are, in general, more successful because they are more contained. From its inception in 1976, this New York based, illustrated quarterly "Magazine of Myth and Tradition" has been aimed at a general, educated readership. A Consulting Editor since the beginning, Travers has contributed short essays and reviews (of approximately 2000 words, on average) to almost every theme oriented issue. *What the Bee Knows* (1989) is a recently published selection of these essays and stories.

She constantly celebrates myth as an interior mode that allows us to rediscover our own identities. An attitude of receptivity and eagerness is essential to the unfolding of this process. As Travers explains, "in order to understand, I come to something with my unknowing—my nakedness, if you like: I stand under it and let it teach me, rain down its truth upon me" (1.1.1976, 46). All first person divulgences, her essays retain a sense of imminence and vulnerability. Contemplating the "ever-germinating myth" of the Dreamtime leads her to exhort readers "to become our own ancestors, . . . [to] waken the images, absorb their ambivalent power and explore them in ourselves—cannibal, totem and taboo, the wild man and the sage" (2.2.1977, 17). Although we may hear echoes of Claude Levi-Strauss, Mircea Eliade and Joseph Campbell, Travers' voice is distinct, characterized by the directness and fervor of a believer in the omnipresence of myth. A conversation with the archaeologist Michael Dames about the monuments at Avebury and Silbury, prompts her observations about the underlying sacredness and femininity of these tellurian temples: "in a sense, we're in the Great Mother; and alternately, the Great

Mother is in us" (3.1.1978, 87). This paradox, of being contained and container, is an idiosyncratic trait of her response to myth: "that to be vulnerable, naked and defenseless is the only way to safety; that the sieve knows a lot about water, emptiness of plenitude, the Eryness of kindliness" (3.4.1978, 61). Letting meaning discover us, she later affirms, places us in the necessarily dualistic, but not always comfortable, position of seeing good and ill, white and black, preservers and destroyers. Travers credits such a mythic "style of thinking" on "this primordial theme" with the origin of the "Happy Ever After" chapter of *Mary Poppins Opens the Door,* which she describes as taking down "at the dictation of the bees," ancient symbols of life (6.1.1981, 46–47).

Travers' essays on fairy tale are largely devoted to explaining and defending the character of the youngest brother, the so called fool or simpleton. She disagrees with Bruno Bettelheim's assessment of the "silly fellow," and instead elevates this figure as "the one who is blessed with Unknowing" (1.3.1976, 114). Later she traces the features of the simpleton in the Hanged Man of the Tarot deck who, being "set free of his too-much knowledge," swings "between Nonexistence and Existence" (9.1.1984, 47). Her essay, "The Youngest Brother," speculates that the character's "celestial shrewdness" might represent the highest achievement of one developing individual, which follows from her suggestion that the three brothers may, in fact, be "a threefold composite of one man, three stages in a single life" (4.1.1979, 38, 42). Travers' love of the fairy tale, though fostered over a considerable span of years, still preserves a fresh, unsophisticated openness, a trait she illustrates through a charming vignette from her childhood. A laundress named Matilda would regale her with stories called "grims," which the pre-literate Travers "took . . . as a generic term for narrative, taradiddle, story"; only when she began to recognize letters did she make the connection between Jakob and Wilhelm Grimm, and Matilda's "social currency" (4.3.1979, 88). Yet, that blood-curdling delight and horror are exactly the response "the Primary World" of fairy tale should call forth. "In order to go on living: it needs . . . the things man cannot create—the earth with all its composted dead, the rain that raineth every day, the seasons, nightfall, silence—and an ear free from all pulsation but that of its own blood" (94).

The stories she has composed for *Parabola* offer more glimpses of her childhood and more elucidations of her own theories. Issued in 1980 as a picture book illustrated by Leo and Diane Dillon, Travers' "Two Pairs of Shoes" first appeared in *Parabola* (1.3.1976, 68–73). It consisted of "Abu Kassem's Slippers" retold from the Thamarat Ul-Awrak (Fruit of Leaves) of Ibn Hijjat Al-Hamawi and "The Sandals of Ayaz" from the Mathnawi of Jalal-u'ddin Rumi. A study in contrasting temperaments, the two part Near Eastern story develops two different views of wealth and service. The first tells of a rich miser reduced to penury because of his unwillingness, and inability, to rid himself of a pair of decrepit slippers. The hero of the second is King Mahmud's obedient treasurer, Ayaz, who, Daniel-like, in the face of the intrigues of his courtly peers, remains faithful to his humble beginnings, represented by his own tattered sandals. Although the setting is similar to that of "Sleeping Beauty," Travers' style in "Two Pairs of Shoes" is the furthest thing from clutter or flummery. Clipped, precise, and believable, the narrative moves with an inexorable but unselfconscious rapidity. In "The Garment," she relies on another contrasting strategy, recalling the stages in the life of a man seeking entry to heaven (10.4.1985, 24–27). The supplicant's progress—from presenting himself in a shining, spotless garment, which can be "read . . . as though it were a book," to appearing in rags whose very threadbareness indicates that he is emptied of all that he was—supplies his passport to a truly Pauline journey of discovery, temptation, fallibility, and grief. Her own past is never far away from these *Parabola* fables. In a conversation with Laurens van der Post, she reveals a rather cryptic appraisal of the need to revise the "Bad Tuesday" chapter "by removing the heart from one of the Mary Poppins stories and transplanting another" (7.2.1982, 39). Her contribution to "A Parabola Bestiary," on the subject of the cow, refers to "the sacred mother animal that lets down milk for man" and to leaning "a cheek against that skiey flank" (8.2.1983, 39, 40), with a vocabulary that recalls the scene of young love in her "Prayer in a Field," published over half a century earlier.

Many of Travers' essays begin as descriptions or vignettes and quickly become visionary conjectures, doors into other dimensions and times. Sitting in Brompton graveyard; walking the maze at Chartres; kneeling before another woman on the tatami of a Japanese inn; listening to the frustrations of a surly nineteen-year-old girl; submitting to an interviewer's questions—all these events trigger thoughts about her own life and the mysterious links between past and present. The narrative transitions of her essays, their hinges, are entirely self styled.

Resting in the Brompton graveyard catapults her back to the Australian church graveyard where she and her siblings, having been set free before the sermon, busy themselves rearranging the flowers. "From graves that still had friends to tend them, we took cut flowers from the pannikins and doled them out, just rather than merciful, to those that had been forgotten" (2.1.1977, 6). Returning to the present, she contemplates a different kind of exchange, involving the child whose birth is awaited in a home nearby. Addressing her final words to this infant, "still swinging in [its] veiny hammock," she formulates a request that summarizes her meditation on the paradoxes of life and death: "pray for me now and at the hour of my birth" (9).

Travers' parabolist tendencies lead to "a kind of unravelling, not so much a discovering as an uncovering of secret things."[13] She describes the experience of walking the maze at Chartres as a discovery of the labyrinth of her self: "through the sweet that so soon becomes the bitter; the taking of what is not one's own, the discarding of that which should be grasped" (8.1.1983, 25). A less predictable connection emerges from her encounter with the Japanese woman. When this stranger in a yukata ventures, haltingly, to explain that "A-Wa-Re" means "The Pity of Things" in her tongue, Travers draws the parallel with the English word, *aware,* which often implies the Japanese meaning as a consequence and which occurs for her, fittingly, in the Irish ejaculation "Ah my grief" (12.4.1987, 20).

Clarifying her sympathy with the teenager's discontent leads Travers to expand—through more images—her ideals of reconciliation and nonseparation. She sees herself slithering between conformity and non-conformity "like the Argonauts through the Clashing Rocks," being in a constant state of "readiness" with the "need to go widdershins round my mind, stand on my head, as it were" (13.2.1988, 38).

Depending on the reader's own point of view, Travers can appear either singularly unprepared for, or cannily responsive to, the interviewer's insistent question about the source of the stories with which she reportedly entertained her younger siblings. A poignant revelation results, however, about the ten-year-old comforting these children, while her recently widowed mother, "her blue robe hanging from her shoulders, hair in a walnut braid down her back, her face white and distraught" (13.1.1988, 81), bursts out of the house to walk in the rain storm. Travers as a grown woman attempting reconciliation realizes her mother's sense of loss, and belatedly extends a comforting hand. At eighty-two she recalls the child she was, "as green and tightly folded as a bud on a winter branch, not knowing what would later ripen; what woman-stuff, now in embryo, would comprehend the inner ferment that tonight had clearly reached its climax and urged her out into the storm" (81). She counterpoints this tight in-turning with a desire to reach out and commiserate, a desire expressed through describing a piece of furniture. "The bed, once proportionate to conjugal life with its whispered sleepy confabulations; . . . naked foot over naked foot, the day dissolved, absolved by the night—was now as wide as a desert. . . . Fulness had become emptiness" (84).

Among the most engaging of Travers' essays are those which, without resorting to any contemporary event or pretext, reanimate scenes from her childhood. The perspective is that of the adult looking back. The sense of disclosure and drama is writerly. But for all these marks of the professional, such essays as "Name and No Name" (7.3.1982, 42–46) and "Miss Quigley" (9.2.1984, 73–75) preserve a certain ingenuousness which takes the reader directly into the world of the child. The earlier piece meditates on the name, as a power that binds but separates, distinguishes but should not be considered familiar, along with a recollection of her own fear at having to stand and declare herself in answer to the Catechism question"What is your name?". Trembling because her name fit none of the suggested rubrics ("'N. or M.,' it said."), she deduces that her father, like the Miller in "Rumplestiltskin," will have to palm her off with a false boast as either N. or M. "in order to jockey [her] into heaven" (42). Yet further consideration lets her remember the primacy of naming in that tale and, steeled with such knowledge, she declares herself in an answer whose implications she continues to ponder. "I [was] given an identity, made object to some subject that might or might not be someday known. No longer one with the grass and the hare, I felt the mystery of the name, the obligation, the danger" (43–44). A blend of childlike intuition and philosophical retrospection infuses her account of a foray into the yard of a neighbouring spinster to steal apples. The children's perception of Miss Quigley's broken heart, "like a Dresden cup . . . shattering against the wall of her bosom" (73), is dangerously close to coyness. But their reaction to her hospitable greeting and invitation to listen to her music box is believable enough; it undoes all the young robbers' resolve to conceal the spoils inside their clothing. As enchanted and dreamy as they become with the music, though, they abruptly switch moods when their hostess kindly provides them with bags for the apples. Feeling "cheated" at having their booty turned into a gift, the children turn the tables and judge Miss Quigley the thief, "slipping a hand into Cause's pocket to steal away Effect" (75). The children's disappointment in Miss Quigley's good intentions, although it might seem remarkably mature (or, for some, ungrateful) on their part, nonetheless bears strong witness to Travers' own desire for complete experience without interruption or attenuation. "No robber worth his salt will lightly be party to forgiveness before it is wanted or asked for" (75).

Travers' essays leave the reader with a sense of a writer, both amazingly vulnerable and strongly opinionated, engaged in a lifelong "mental fight" (13.3.1988, 32). More divagations than rigorous expositions, her pieces are associative and rambling. They hold unknowing, emptiness, and openness above knowledge, full-ness, and closure. They eschew "what the world calls common sense, that popular lumpen wisdom that prevents the emerging of the numinous" (10.3.1985, 78). In its place they support a globe-circling consciousness, oblivious of time and constraint. As Travers proclaims, "I have been at the dark corroboree where the feet of men make a drum of the earth and heard them call to the Rainbow Snake to take them into the Dreaming" (11.4.1986, 34). Through all her seekings and findings she looks and longs for "something else," but admits that her own glosses of transcen-dence and "that homesickness of my childhood" (13.3.1988, 31) are inadequate to explain all that the term comprehends. In the same essay, she describes the effects of this questing on the body and the heart. As in all her *Parabola* work, the point is not to separate external from internal, but to suggest their connected-ness. "Thus the body, that essential alchemical vessel in which, through the affinity of its functions, the question must first have arisen, begins to receive—oh, visitations, unwonted physical impressions, parables, as it were, of the senses, that wordlessly convey their meaning to essence, mind, and heart" (31).

8

"Dear Fly!": Toward a
View of P. L. Travers

I met P. L. Travers on a Saturday afternoon in June 1988. After battling contingents of rainbow-headed punkers and elbowing shoppers on the King's Road, it was a pleasure to turn down a quiet Chelsea street, and clap the knocker on the bright pink door, which seemed the perfect backdrop for the pot of blue flowers on the step. We talked in her living room, where the walls themselves provided a cultural commentary—from the Paul Klee painting of a fish; the Eileen Agar drawing of Travers at work in the garden, the frontispiece, which she thinks "should do for me when I'm ninety"; AE's sketch of the young, pensive Travers sitting in a tree; the terracotta bust of an angel with its gold leaf and paint flaking; the oriental calligraphs propped up next to "family" photographs on the mantel; to a bookcase housing well worn children's books and toys. During our observations on Thomas Traherne and Meister Eckhart, however, a pesky fly kept diving at us, until Travers, in midsentence, jumped from the couch and announced that she must get "him" out of the room. After sweeping her arms and cajoling "dear fly" to go away, she returned to the couch, informed me that "no fly is ever killed in this house," and completed her sentence. Although I tried hard to block out the image of Forster's Mrs. Moore, Travers' concern, that this insect who had "been bothering [her] for days" not be harmed, has stayed with me as the dominant impression of the interview, and expression of the woman. She would probably prefer to be seen as a bee, but Travers, the shielder of flies, is for me a protector of life in all forms.

The session, at which inquiry into her "personal or private life" was forbidden, offered more confirmation than information. In a manner both gracious and precise, and in a voice both diffident and full of a raconteur's delight, Travers nodded at the linkages which I mentioned as threading together all her writing. But she registered some trepidation when I kept referring to her "work." "Who am I? A very small little clarinet, not some great Stradivarius." She was surprised that I had unearthed the pieces in the *Irish Statesman* because, as "an innocent," she has "never kept anything." And in reconsidering her review of the Italian pictures, then almost six decades old, she was amazed by "the cheek of it!" Reaffirmations were more numerous than surprises. When I pursued the theme of an author writing to please herself, Travers challenged that the author writes not for some image of her distant child-self, but rather because "the adult still *is* that child," even when, sadly, the child has been "muddied over." In talking about her childhood, Travers described herself as a "dreamy" youngster, "unlike the rest of the family," and credited the "quiet times" alone as educational. Although she feels she knows Mary Poppins "slightly better" than she did five decades ago, Travers considers herself a mere relayer of intimations, gleaned from the character's unpredictable visits. Mary Poppins not only stands in front of the unknown, she is "part of it," and, as always, Travers has "to depend on her." So moved was she in rereading *MPCTL,* now her favorite book of the series, that she rang up the publisher and asked, "Did I write this?" She became especially animated when talking about Mr. Banks, a character of whom she is very fond. "Did you not think," she ventured, "that, when Mr. Banks found himself standing between Mary Poppins and Mrs. Corry, it was almost as though he'd known them before?" I concurred that this was a particularly "moonstruck moment." As I walked back to the King's Road, remembering her strong handshake, awash with ideas and connections, I kept returning to the episode in-

volving Mr. Banks. It struck me as emblematic of the continuous
cycle of return and restoration in Travers' own life.

> Suddenly, Mr. Banks was flooded with a sense of being
> somewhere else. And, also, of being someone else who
> was, at the same time, himself.
> White-collared and velvet suited, he was standing tip-
> toe in button-up boots, his nose just reaching a glass-
> topped counter, over which he was handing to someone
> he could hardly see, a precious threepenny bit. (*MPCTL*
> 70)

Walking up the street, I also realized that even the dead-ends
in the Travers research had proven to be illuminating. Although Mortimer Browning's "Mary Poppins Suite," which
Travers faintly recalled as an instrumental work, remained elusive—after attempts through the British Library, the American
Society of Composers, Authors, and Publishers, the Library of
Congress Copyright Office, and Theodore Presser Music Publishers—I *had* successfully uncovered the Caedmon recorded reading
with Maggie Smith and Robert Stephens, the Pickwick collection
of Mary Poppins songs, and Duke Ellington's syncopated rehash
of the movie score for Reprise. Similarly, I had been tantalized
with the plans to erect a Mary Poppins statue in the Conservatory
Lake area of Central Park. Travers had insisted that it not be a
climbable statue and, although the British artist I. B. Huxley-
Jones had produced a working sketch, the statue itself never ma-
terialized. The reasons impressed me as similar to those for the
failure of the Disney film: trying to materialize the immaterial,
to bring the imaginative down to earth. Specifically, the Park
Commission determined that a nonclimbable statue would not
blend in with the climbable Alice statue and the representation
of Hans Andersen. They felt it would be an invitation to vandals,
and that the depiction itself was aesthetically unpleasing. Arbi-
ters of public taste (in terms of parks, at least) and some screen
writers, I deduced, were strangely similar. What was missing
from this bureaucratic decision making was an appreciation of

the evanescence of Mary Poppins and the protective privacy, which often appears to be prickliness, of P. L. Travers herself.

A description borrowed from one of Travers' first and greatest mentors, AE, elucidates the striking and unifying feature of her work: a strong belief in the dreams and perceptions of childhood, that vale of soul making. His observations on a poor child's house of cinders, tallying nicely with Travers' own childhood pastime of park making, also affirm the lifelong resonances of these apparently fragile undertakings.

> I see a child, a curious, delicate little thing, seated on the doorstep of a house. It is an alley in some great city, and there is a gloom of evening and vapour over the sky. I see the child is bending over the path; he is picking cinders and arranging them, and as I ponder, I become aware that he is laying down in gritty lines the walls of a house, the mansion of his dream. Here spread along the pavement are large rooms, these for his friends, and a tiny room in the centre, that is his own. So his thought plays. Just then I catch a glimpse of the corduroy trousers of a passing workman, and a heavy boot crushes through the cinders. I feel the pain in the child's heart as he shrinks back, his little lovelit house of dreams all rudely shattered. Ah, poor child, building the City Beautiful out of a few cinders, yet nigher, truer in intent than many a stately, gold-rich palace. . . .[1]

Like AE, Travers has never lost her intuitive sympathy with such dreamy times. Her stories assuredly build these dreams with words.

Appendix

A Review by P. L. Travers

"The Hidden Child"
by Milo Reve

In literature there are no infallible recipes. Yet it is possible, by mixing certain established ingredients, for most people to concoct some sort of a novel. And who was it said "As for the poor, let them write their autobiographies!"? There are few who have not once been poets, in the neap-tide of youth; historians, psychologists and philosophers abound in every side street; journalists are ten a penny. But there is one branch of literature that cannot be made successful by any amount of wishing, willing or industrious effort—the writing of books for children. Over a long period, hundreds of years, the books that have survived oblivion and become children's classics can be counted on fingers and toes.

I have before me *The Tale of Beatrix Potter* (admirably and affectionately recorded by Margaret Lane) which corroborates the suspicion I have long held that the secret of the successful children's book is that it is not written for children. It is not even a prime essential that such an author should love and understand children; the fact that he (or she) very often does has no true bearing on the work. Nor is it necessary that he should mix a great deal with the pigmy race that appreciates him. Outside appreciation of any kind is of secondary importance to the true children's writer. For him the first and ultimate requirement is that the book should please himself. For he is the one for whom the book is written. With it he puts to sleep his wakeful youth and tells the story to the hidden child within him. Not consciously, of course, or the tale would lose its effect. He writes, in ignorance and innocence, his primer of magic and wisdom. "My childhood bends beside me" wrote James Joyce in "Ulysses." This is inevitably true of every artist, particularly of the writers of children's books. Such works are more often than not the results of an imaginative mind playing its light over lonely or bitter childhoods. What the child lacked in those tender years the imagination gives back to it. And this retrospective process may go on for book after book until the time comes when the child is appeased and freed. That the tales cease then is not necessarily a sign of failing imagination but rather that the writer has set himself free to find his fate in the grown-up world. This is another version of the story of the ugly duckling, who puts aside his duckling grief when at last he joins the swans.

Beatrix Potter's life is a perfect example of this pattern. Her rigorous Victorian childhood reads like the record of life on an island rock. Year after year, alone in a nursery in Bolton Gardens, she lunched on a daily cutlet and a plate of rice pudding much as a castaway might regale himself from a single clump of lichen. The data we are given is *(sic)* meagre for the good reason that nothing ever happened to her until the age of thirty-six. It was then that she published in book form the illustrated letters she had written to a child years before—*The Tale of Peter Rabbit*. Entranced with the first success she had known in life she followed it up with *The Tailor of Gloucester, Squirrel Nutkin, Benjamin Bunny, Two Bad Mice,* and *Mrs. Tiggy Winkle.* Approaching forty, she engaged herself, against the will of her crustacean parents, to a member of her publishing firm, who died a few months later. This was grief and her undaunted spirit, greedy for experience, took it as a gift. With her first earnings, plus a small legacy, she bought a farm in the Lake District, installed a tenant farmer, and for eight years—snatching a week here and there from the rigours of Bolton Gardens, she built, and pruned, sowed and reaped and poured out the treasures of her heart in a spate of little books. Then, as she herself put it, quoting from *The Tempest,* Spring came to her "at the farthest, in the very end of harvest." She married a country lawyer, put on her swan plumage, laid down her pen and lapsed into happy-ever-after. Full and rich with immediate life she had no overspill for the hidden child; indeed, because of that late fullness the child no longer needed her. She became what she had instinctively longed to be, as much part of the earth as tree and stone and, like tree and stone, she was silent.

There we have the skeleton. And a skeleton articulated with loving care by an author who has left no possible stone unturned, in her search for the facts. What there are of these are recorded with humour and in a neat and succinct style that is worthy of its subject. I think it must have needed intrepidity as well as a talent for noting down essentials to disinter the bones of Beatrix Potter's childhood and make of them the outline of a life. Whatever humanly could be saved from the silence has been effectively rescued by Miss Lane. But however well documented and sympathetically interpreted, they remain bones. For the living flesh of her youthful years we must go to the books themselves. From these emerges a formidable figure, a character whose moral nature was as rugged as her instinctive nature was abundant and her artist nature acute. To begin with she knew exactly what she wanted. Her first glimpse of the countryside, Miss Lane tells us, aroused in her the lifelong passion that became articulate only with the purchase of Hill Top Farm. Forever sketching and drawing from earliest youth, her piercing vision conveyed to accurate hand the minutiae of woods and fields—speedwell, squirrel's eye, mouse's ear, flower of moss—until she was more than well-equipped to illustrate her tales. By surrounding herself continuously with a small menagerie—hedgehog, rabbit, cat, mouse, snails, dogs, minnows—she familiarized herself, in loneliness, with deep instinctive life. "Thank goodness!" she said in later years, "my education was neglected!"—accurately perceiving from what wound her bow was strung. So, fully in possession of her own mind, she was able to insist that her stories should be produced as *she* wanted them and we have her to thank for perpetuating the perfect size in children's books—five inches by four—a proper fit for their readers' hands and pockets. As for the tales themselves, they all fulfil the prime necessities of a nursery classic. Each is built upon some simple everyday happening; it is full of feeling yet without the least hint of sentimentality; it suggests all the magic of the extra-world without ever stooping to explanation; above all, it has an element of danger and suspense, even of terror, that is only dispersed by the joy of the happy ending. We seem to see, in all the tales, the dreadful parents of Bolton Gardens dressed up in many disguises—Mr. MacGregor in *Peter Rabbit,* the cat that sits for five hours on top of the Benjamin Bunny's basket, Old Brown who puts Squirrel Nutkin in his waistcoat pocket and Simpkin, ruthlessly hiding the cherry-coloured twist. All the stories have an underlying irony and a tough, non-nonsense quality that does not shrink from terrible happenings—Jemima Puddleduck in that gloomy wood, which the foxgloves only make more frightful, Mr. Jeremy's moment in the stomach of the trout, and worst of all, the rats turning Tom Kitten into a Roly-Poly pudding.

But Beatrix Potter does not merely fulfil the bare injunctions of the classic. One could become lyrical about the new elements she adds were it not that we are forced, by her own example, to keep our feet on the earth. The beautiful femininity of her female characters, for instance,—their common sense, foresightedness and housewifely sweetness—Hunca Munca paying for her thefts by sweeping out the doll's house; Mrs. Tiggy Winkle, that excellent clear-starcher, with her industry and gentleness; Jemima Puddleduck (the artistic type!) so absent-minded, so bad a sitter yet withal so fondly maternal; Mrs. Tabitha Twitchett, anxious parent, fine cook and a bit of a gossip; and, queen of them all, the neat and tidy, eternally flustered little widow, Mrs. Tittlemouse.

There are, too, those rare delicious moments when the author of the Tales allows herself to be tempted into the script. "They had roasted grass-hopper with lady-bird sauce which frogs consider a beautiful treat but *I* (she really cannot resist it!) *I* think it must have been nasty!" The rats in *The Roly-Poly Pudding* carry off their bundles on a little wheel-barrow "which looked very like mine . . . and I'm sure *I* never gave them leave to borrow my wheel-barrow!" And again, she protests, *she* has seen the door leading into "that hill called Cat-bells—and besides *I* am very well acquainted with Mrs. Tiggy Winkle!" That dominant *I* insisting and declaring, claiming to be always right and brooking no contradiction—how perfect and apt it is. For in the children's world there must be no uncertainties, no might-be, maybe cloud of grey but only the solidest black and white.

The best of the books, which means most of them, are as direct and bare and complete as a lyric. The art of them is continually fresh with nothing ever too much. "The boat was round and green and very like other lily-leaves" she tells us, packing imagination and precision together. Mr. Jackson "was sitting all over a small rocking-chair," in Mrs. Tittlemouse's parlour. "Let us" says the fox to Jemima, "have a little dinner-party all to ourselves!" What infinite worlds these phrases are, each bounded in a nutshell.

But of all her qualities, the rarest seems to me the sudden wild and gay inconsequence that occasionally seizes her and wafts her into a mad and beautiful, almost surrealist, dream where everything is a non-sequitur. The duck, putting on Tom Kitten's clothes and finding them a very bad fit, remarks unexpectedly but somehow with absolute rightness "It's a very fine morning said Mr. Drake Puddleduck." Mr. John Dormouse, being complained to about some matter, "stayed in bed and would say nothing but "very snug' which is not the way to carry on a retail business." And Mr. Jackson, that unwelcome but determined guest, prefaces, for no other reason but the fun of it, each outrageous demand for food with"Tiddly, widdly, widdly!"

There is a curious mixture of simplicity and extreme deliberation in Beatrix Potter's writing. As far as the stories are concerned she seems to have been continually aware of herself as artist. "I think I write carefully (Miss Lane quotes her) because I enjoy my writing and enjoy taking pains over it. I have always disliked writing to order; I write to please myself. . . . My usual way of writing is to scribble and cut out and write it again and again. The shorter and plainer the better. And read the Bible (unrevised version and Old Testament) if I feel my style wants chastening." Admirable recipe! She appears less convinced, however, of the value of those minute masterpieces that are the illustrations. With that formidable cantankerousness that developed as she grew older she would retort—again I quote Miss Lane—"Great rubbish!" or "Absolute bosh!" when anyone praised them highly. But the fact remains that they were then and still are—think of Timmy Willie asleep in the pea-pod!—as unique and unmatchable as the stories themselves, and as traditionally and superbly English. She was in both worlds an artist beyond compare. Others have tried to fly in her particular patch of sky but they do not stay the course not only, perhaps, because they are dimmer of eye and drabber of feather but because they lack her imagination and her lonely childhood that carved such a hardy channel for it. She rose like a phoenix from her youth and to match the lustre of her living art you must find such another bird.

Notes and References

Chapter One

1. P. L. Travers, "Give the Kid a Bible, for Instance," *Esquire* 85, no. 3 (1976): 86.

2. Richard Lingeman, "Visit with Mary Poppins and P. L. Travers," *New York Times Magazine,* 25 December 1966, 25; Roy Newquist, *Conversations* (Chicago: Rand McNally, 1967), 432.

3. Joseph Roddy, "A Visit with the Real Mary Poppins," *Look,* 13 December 1966, 84.

4. P. L. Travers,"Where Did She Come From? Why Did She Go?," *Saturday Evening Post,* 7 November 1964, 78.

5. Roddy, "A Visit," 85; Edwina Burness and Jerry Griswold, "The Art of Fiction LXXIII: P. L. Travers," *Paris Review* 86 (1982): 214.

6. Jonathan Cott, *Pipers at the Gates of Dawn* (New York: Random House, 1983), 227.

7. Neil Philip, "The Writer and the Nanny Who Never Explain," *Times Educational Supplement,* 11 June 1982, 42; Janet Graham, "The Cup of Sorrow in Every Woman's Life," *Ladies' Home Journal* 84, no. 2 (1967): 68.

8. P. L. Travers, "A Radical Innocence," *New York Times Book Review,* 9 May 1965, 1; P. L. Travers, "A Kind of Visitation," in *Randall Jarrell 1914–1965,* ed. R. Lowell et al. (New York: Farrar, Straus & Giroux, 1967), 254.

9. P. L. Travers; "The Heroes of Childhood; A Note on Nannies," *Horn Book* 11 (1935): 150.

10. Travers, "Give the Kid a Bible," 150.

11. Graham, "The Cup of Sorrow," 68.

12. Travers, "A Radical Innocence," 1.

13. P. L. Travers, "Autobiographical Sketch," in *The Junior Book of Authors,* ed. S. J. Kunitz and H. Haycraft (New York: H. W. Wilson, 1951), 287.

14. Graham, "The Cup of Sorrow," 70.

15. P. L. Travers, "Only Connect," in *Only Connect; Readings on Children's Literature,* ed. S. Egoff et al. (Toronto: Oxford University Press, 1969), 184.

16. Lingeman, "Visit," 29.

17. Travers, "A Radical Innocence," 39.

18. P. L. Travers, "Who Is Mary Poppins?," *Junior Bookshelf* 18 (1954): 47; Travers, "Where Did She Come From?," 78.

19. Travers, "The Heroes of Childhood," 150.

20. *Ibid.,* 154.

21. Travers, "Where Did She Come From?," 78.

22. Travers, "Only Connect," 187.

23. P. L. Travers, "My Childhood Bends Beside Me," *New Statesman and Nation,* 29 November 1952, 839.

24. P. L. Travers, "Grimm's," *New Republic,* 25 December 1944, 873–74.

25. P. L. Travers, "The Black Sheep," *New York Times Book Review,* 7 November 1965, 61.

26. P. L. Travers, "Once I Saw a Fox Dancing Alone," *New York Herald Tribune Book Week,* 9 May 1965, 2.

27. Newquist, *Conversations,* 425.

28. Michele Field, "Reminiscing with P. L. Travers," *Publishers Weekly,* 21 March 1986, 41.

29. Travers, "Only Connect," 193.

30. P. L. Travers, "The Death of AE: Irish Hero and Mystic," in *The Celtic Consciousness,* ed. R. O'Driscoll (New York: Braziller, 1982), 476, 472.

31. Ibid., 472, 473.

32. AE, *An Essay on the Character in Irish Literature* (Dublin: The Cuala Press, 1932), unpaginated.

33. AE, *Selected Poems* (London: Macmillan, 1935), 179.

34. Newquist, *Conversations,* 426–27.

35. Burness and Griswold, "The Art of Fiction," 227.

36. Roddy, "A Visit," 85; P. L. Travers, "In Search of the Hero; The Continuing Relevance of Myth and Fairy Tale," *Scripps College Bulletin* XLIV. no. 3 (1970): unpaginated.

37. P. L. Travers, "On Not Writing for Children," *Children's Literature* 4 (1975).

38. P. L. Travers, "Foreword," in Rene Zuber, *Who Are You Monsieur Gurdjieff?,* trans. J. Koralek (London: Routledge & Kegan Paul, 1080), vii; Karlfried Graf Durckheim, "The Call for the Master," *Parabola* 14, no. 2 (1989): 6.

Chapter Two

1. Classic essays by W. K. Wimsatt and L. C. Knights warn against imputing intentions to authors and hypothesizing on the flimsi-

est of evidence about their private lives. See W. K. Wimsatt, "The Intentional Fallacy," *Sewanee Review* 54 (1946) and L. C. Knights "How Many Children Had Lady Macbeth?," *Explorations* (1933).

2. Jean-Paul Sartre, *Search for a Method* (New York: Knopf, 1967), 142–43).

3. Julia Kristeva, *Desire in Language; A Semiotic Approach to Literature and Art,* trans. T. Gora et al. (New York: Columbia University Press, 1980), 104.

4. Ibid., 106.

5. Josephine Donovan, "Toward a Women's Poetics," in *Feminist Issues in Literary Scholarship,* ed. S. Benstock (Bloomington: Indiana University Press, 1987), 99.

6. Ibid., 100–104.

7. Lawrence Lipking, "Aristotle's Sister: A Poetics of Abandonment," *Critical Inquiry* 10 (1983): 78.

8. Nina Auerbach, "Engorging the Patriarchy," in *Feminist Issues in Literary Scholarship,* 159.

9. Virginia Woolf, *The Pargiters,* ed. M. Leaska (London: Hogarth Press, 1978), xxxvii–xxxviii.

Chapter Three

1. P. L. Travers, *Moscow Excursion* (London: Gerald Howe, 1934), 6–7; hereafter cited in the text.

2. McLuskie, "The Patriarchal Bard," in *Political Shakespeare,* ed. J. Dollimore (Manchester: University of Manchester Press, 1985), 88–108; P. Erickson, *Patriarchal Structures in Shakespeare's Drama* (Berkeley: University of California Press, 1985); E. Showalter, "Representing Ophelia: Women, Madness, and the Responsibilities of Feminist Criticism," in *Shakespeare and the Question of Theory,* ed. P. Parker (New Haven: Yale University Press, 1985), 75–99; M. Sprengnether, "Annihilating Intimacy in *Coriolanus,*" in *Women in the Middle Ages and the Renaissance,* ed. M. B. Rose (Syracuse: Syracuse University Press, 1986), 89–112.

3. P. L. Travers, *Mary Poppins in the Park* (New York: Harcourt, Brace, 1952), 22, 21; hereafter cited in the text.

Chapter Four

Note: Quotations from the first four Mary Poppins books will be based on the Harcourt Brace Jovanovich Voyager Books editions.

1. P. L. Travers, *Happy Ever After,* illus. Mary Shepard (New York: Reynal & Hitchcock, 1940), 19; hereafter cited in the text.

2. P. L. Travers, *Aunt Sass* (New York: Reynal & Hitchcock, 1941), 32, 11; hereafter cited in the text.

3. P. L., Travers, *Johnny Delaney* (New York: High Grade Press, 1944), 7; hereafter cited in the text.

4. P. L. Travers, *Ah Wong* (New York: High Grade Press, 1943), 16; hereafter cited in the text.

5. P. L. Travers, *Mary Poppins Opens the Door,* illus. M. Shepard and A. Sims (New York: Reynal & Hitchcock, 1943), 176; hereafter cited in the text.

6. Iona and Peter Opie, eds. *The Oxford Dictionary of Nursery Rhymes* (Oxford: At the Clarendon Press, 1951), 337–39.

7. P. L. Travers, *I Go by Sea, I Go by Land,* illus. G. Hermes (New York: W. W. Norton, 1941), 232; hereafter cited in the text.

8. P. L. Travers, *Mary Poppins Comes Back,* illus. M. Shepard (New York: Harcourt, Brace, 1935), 120; hereafter cited in the text.

9. P. L. Travers, *The Fox at the Manger* (London: Collins, 1963), 70–71; hereafter cited in the text.

Chapter Five

1. *Mary Poppins in the Park,* 188; the speaker, significantly, is Mr. Banks.

2. Roger L. Green, *Tellers of Tales; Children's Books and Their Authors* (London: Kaye & Ward,1969), 273.

3. Evelyn Waugh, *A Handful of Dust* (London: Chapman & Hall, 1934), 27.

4. Jonathan Gathorne-Hardy, *The Unnatural History of the Nanny* (New York: The Dial Press, 1973), 309.

5. P. L. Travers, *Mary Poppins, Revised Edition,* illus. M. Shepard (New York: Harcourt Brace Jovanovich, 1981), 3–4.

6. Louise Irvine, *Royal Doulton Series Ware,* 3 vols. (London: Richard Dennis, 1986), 3: 63.

7. I. and P. Opie, *The Oxford Dictionary of Nursery Rhymes,* 69–70.

8. Cott, *Pipers at the Gates of Dawn,* 195.

9. E. Hennecke and W. Schneemelcher, eds., *New Testament Apocrypha,* 2 vols. (London: Lutterworth, 1965), 2:228.

10. George Edward Farrow, *The Wallypug of Why* (London: Hutchinson, 1895), 59, 86, 158.

11. Humphrey Carpenter and Mari Prichard, *The Oxford Compan-*

ion to Children's Literature (New York: Oxford University Press, 1984), 342; Humphrey Carpenter, "Mary Poppins, Force of Nature," *New York Times Book Review,* 27 August 1989, 29.

12. Perry Nodelman, "Introduction: On Words and Pictures, Neglected Noteworthies, and Touchstones in Training," *Touchstones: Reflections on the Best in Children's Literature,* ed. P. Nodelman, 3 vols. (Purdue University: Children's Literature Association, 1989), 3:8–9

13. Laura Hoffeld, "Where Magic Begins," *The Lion and the Unicorn* 3 (1979): 9.

14. Staffan Bergsten, *Mary Poppins and Myth* (Stockholm: Almquist & Wiksell International, 1978), 71.

15. Cott, *Pipers at the Gates of Dawn,* 236.

16. Kenneth J. Reckford, *Aristophanes' Old-and-New Comedy* (Chapel Hill: University of North Carolina Press, 1987), 103–4.

17. Newquist, *Conversations,* 429.

18. Peter and Dorothy Bart, "As Told and Sold by Disney," *New York Times Book Review,* 9 May 1965, 2, 34.

19. Rosemary Smith, "Walt Disney's *Mary Poppins,*" *Elementary English* 44 (1967): 29, 30.

20. Travers, "Only Connect," 194.

21. Feenie Ziner, "Mary Poppins as a Zen Monk," *New York Times Book Review,* 7 May 1972, 2.

22. Cott, *Pipers at the Gates of Dawn,* 219.

Chapter Six

1. P. L. Travers, *Mary Poppins in Cherry Tree Lane* (London: Collins, 1982), 71; hereafter cited in the text.

2. Humphrey Carpenter, "Mary Poppins, Force of Nature," *New York Times Book Review,* 27 August 1989, 29.

3. P. L. Travers, *Mary Poppins and the House Next Door,* illus. M. Shepard (London: Collins, 1988), 60, 63; hereafter cited in the text.

4. Anne Carroll Moore, "Mary Poppins," *Horn Book* 11 (1935): 7.

5. John Rowe Townsend, *Written for Children; An Outline of English-language Children's Literature* (London: Garnet Miller, 1965), 176; Jane Yolen, "Makers of Modern Myths," *Horn Book* 51 (1975): 496.

6. Albert V. Schwartz, "*Mary Poppins* Revised: An Interview with P. L. Travers," *Interracial Books for Children* 5 (1974): 5.

7. Robert B. Moore, "A Letter from a Critic," *Children's Literature* 10 (1982): 212–13.

8. Schwartz, "Interview," 3.

9. Ibid., 1.

10. P. L. Travers, "A Letter from the Author, *Children's Literature* 10 (1982): 216–17.

11. P. L. Travers, *Mary Poppins,* illus. Mary Shepard (New York: Reynal & Hitchcock, 1934), 92, 97.

12. Jim Brady, "Mother Goose Plucked Clean," *The Globe and Mail,* 21 January 1989, C-1.

Chapter Seven

1. Cott, *Pipers at the Gates of Dawn,* 215.

2. Paul Heins, "P. L. Travers, *Friend Monkey," Horn Book* 48 (1972): 53–54.

3. Travers' writings in *Parabola* are listed by volume, number, and year, followed by page numbers. The bibliography contains a complete list of titles, chronologically arranged.

4. Cott, *Pipers at the Gates of Dawn,* 214.

5. P. L. Travers, *Friend Monkey,* illus. C. Keeping (New York: Harcourt Brace Jovanovich, 1971), 96; hereafter cited in the text.

6. Cott, *Pipers at the Gates of Dawn,* 216.

7. "P. L. Travers' *About the Sleeping Beauty," Kirkus Reviews,* 15 October 1975, 1202.

8. Jonathan Cott, *"About the Sleeping Beauty," New York Times Book Review,* 28 September 1975, 27–28.

9. Michael Patrick Hearn, "P. L. Travers in Fantasy Land," *Children's Literature* 6 (1977): 223–24.

10. Joseph Cary, "Six Beauties Sleeping," *Children's Literature* 6 (1977): 231, 233.

11. Hearn, "P. L. Travers in Fantasy Land," 224; Cary, "Six Beauties Sleeping," 233.

12. P. L. Travers, *About the Sleeping Beauty,* illus. Charles Keeping (New York: McGraw-Hill, 1975), 53; hereafter cited in the text.

13. P. L. Travers, "Foreword," René Zuber, *Who Are You Monsieur Gurdjieff?* (London: Routledge & Kegan Paul, 1980), vii.

Chapter Eight

1. AE, *The Hero in Man* (London: Orpheus Press, 1909), 18.

Selected Bibliography

Primary Sources

A Note on Editions of Mary Poppins and on Periodicals

In most cases the Mary Poppins books have been published simultaneously in London and New York. The first London publishers were Gerald Howe (1934) and Lovat Dickson & Thompson (1935); in the fifties and sixties the London publishers were Peter Davies and Collins. The American publishers have been Reynal & Hitchcock and Harcourt, Brace. Recent books and reissues have been published by Collins, Harcourt Brace Jovanovich (Voyager Books), and Delacorte. My citations come most often from first American editions.

I have consulted the complete runs of the two periodicals cited extensively in Chapters Two and Three, the *Irish Statesman* (1923–30) and the *New English Weekly* (1932–49), in the Colindale Branch of the British Library. For ease of reference I have identified each of Travers' contributions in chronological order by date and page; I have used the same system to list her work in *Parabola* (1976–).

1. Novels and Stories

About the Sleeping Beauty. Illustrated by Charles Keeping. New York: McGraw-Hill, 1975.

Ah Wong. New York: High Grade Press, 1943.

Aunt Sass. New York: Reyal & Hitchcock, 1941.

The Fox at the Manger. Wood engravings by Thomas Bewick. London: Collins, 1963.

Friend Monkey. Illustrated by Charles Keeping. New York: Harcourt Brace Jovanovich, 1971.

Happy Ever After. Illustrated by Mary Shepard. New York: Reynal & Hitchcock, 1940.

I Go by Sea, I Go by Land. Illustrated by Gertrude Hermes. New York: W. W. Norton, 1941.

Johnny Delaney. New York: High Grade Press, 1944.

Maria Poppina ab A ad Z. Picturas delineavit Mary Shepard. Latine reddidit G. M. Lyne. New York: Harcourt Brace & World, 1968.

Mary Poppins. Illustrated by Mary Shepard. New York: Reynal & Hitchcock, 1934.

Mary Poppins. Illustrated by Mary Shepard. Rev. ed. New York: Harcourt Brace Jovanovich, 1981.

Mary Poppins and the House Next Door. Illustrated by Mary Shepard. London: Collins, 1988.

Mary Poppins Comes Back. Illustrated by Mary Shepard. New York: Harcourt, Brace, 1935.

Mary Poppins from A to Z. Illustrated by Mary Shepard. London: Collins, 1962.

Mary Poppins in Cherry Tree Lane. Illustrated by Mary Shepard. London: Collins, 1982.

Mary Poppins in the Kitchen; A Cookery Book with a Story. Illustrated by Mary Shepard. New York: Harcourt Brace Jovanovich, 1975.

Mary Poppins in the Park. Illustrated by Mary Shepard. New York: Harcourt, Brace & World, 1952.

Mary Poppins Opens the Door. Illustrated by Mary Shepard and Agnes Sims. New York: Harcourt, Brace, 1943.

A Mary Poppins Story for Coloring. Illustrated by Mary Shepard. New York: Harcourt Brace Jovanovich, 1969.

Moscow Excursion. London: Gerald Howe, 1934.

Two Pairs of Shoes. Illustrated by Leo and Diane Dillon. New York: Viking Press, 1980.

What the Bee Knows; Reflections on Myth, Symbol and Story. Wellingborough, Northamptonshire: Aquarian Press, 1989.

2. Essays, Poetry, Criticism, and Interviews

"Ah Wong." *Mademoiselle* 9 (November 1943): 82–83, 142–46, 149–50.

"Autobiographical Sketch." In *The Junior Book of Authors,* edited by S. J. Kunitz and H. Haycraft. New York: H. W. Wilson, 1951.

"The Black Sheep." *New York Times Book Review,* 7 November 1965, 1, 61.

"The Death of AE: Irish Hero and Mystic." In *The Celtic Consciousness,* edited by Robert O'Driscoll. New York: Braziller, 1982.

"Foreword," René Zuber, *Who Are You Monsieur Gurdjieff?* Translated by J. Koralek. London: Routledge & Kegan Paul, 1980.

"Give the Kid a Bible, for Instance." *Esquire* 85 no. 3 (March 1976): 86, 149–50.

"Grimm's." *New Republic,* 25 December 1944, 873–74.

"Grimm's Women." *New York Times Book Review,* 16 November 1965, 45.

George Ivanovitch Gurdjieff. Toronto: Traditional Studies Press, 1973.

"The Heroes of Childhood; A Note on Nannies." *Horn Book* 11 (May–June 1935): 147–55.

"In Search of the Hero; The Continuing Relevance of Myth and Fairy Tale," *Scripps College Bulletin* 44, no. 3 (March 1970), unpaginated.

In the *Irish Statesman:* "Christopher," 4 April 1925, 109; "The Coming," 18 July 1925, 587; "Te Deum of a Lark," 7 November 1925, 267; "Happy Sleeping," 27 March 1926, 66; "Oh, Break Her Heart," 5 June 1926, 348; "Ghosts of Two Sad Lovers," 9 October 1926, 104; "On Ben Bulbain," 18 December 1926, 349; "The Dark Fortnight," 29 January 1927, 497; "The Plane Tree," 23 April 1927, 158; "No More Eagles," 9 July 1927, 420; "Phyllida," 29 October 1927, 176; "The Poet," 17 December 1927, 345; "Prayer in a Field," 25 February 1928, 557; "Coming Towards Meadows," 17 November 1928, 208; "The Marbles at Carrara," 12 October 1929, 106–108; "The Apple Cart," 26 October 1929, 152, 154; "The Italian Pictures," 25 January 1930, 412–13; "The Other Side of the Penny," 15 February 1930, 475–77; "A Brand for the Critic," 12 April 1930, 107–8.

"A Kind of Visitation." In *Randall Jarrell 1914–1965,* edited by R. Lowell, P. Taylor, R. Penn Warren. New York: Farrar, Straus & Giroux, 1967.

"A Letter from the Author." *Children's Literature,* 10 (1982): 214–17.

"My Childhood Bends Beside Me." *New Statesman and Nation,* 29 November 1952, 639.

In the *New English Weekly:* "Zodiac Circus," 11 January 1934, 298; "In Time of Trouble," 25 January 1934, 355; "The Tempest (The Old Vic)," 15 February 1934, 423–24; "Elisabeth Bergner," 22 February 1934, 446–47; "Sun in Cancer," 1 March 1934, 475; "Song in Season," 29 March 1934, 565; "Birds in the Hand," 2 May 1935, 56; "American Ghosts,," 4 July 1935, 236; "The Dark Heart," 26 March 1936, 480; "Fulgens and Lucrece," 2 April 1936, 498; "Tonight at Eight-Thirty," 16 April 1936, 13–14; "Sadlers Wells. King Lear," 7 May 1936, 76; "Parnell," 14 May 1936) 94; "Peer Gynt," 21 May 1936, 115–16; "Chastity, My Brother," 28 May 1936, 135; "The Magic Flute in Sussex," 11 June 1936, 173–74; "The Seagull, The Play Produced by Komisarjevsky," 18 June 1936, 194–95; "'The Fugitives,' Apollo Theatre," 25 June 1936, 214–15; "The Insect Play," 9 July 1936, 253; "'After October,'" 16 July 1936, 275; "The Tempest," 23 July 1936, 292; "Twelfth Night at Stratford," 24 September 1936, 394–95; "The Taming of the Shrew," 15 April 1937, 13–14; "Jane Eyre," 22 April 1937, 34; "Lord Adrian," 29 April 1937, 54–55; "Anna Christie," 6

38; "They Walk Alone," 2 February 1939, 254–55; "Two Revivals," 16 February 1939, 287–88; "On the Frontier," 23 February 1939, 302–3; "Johnson Over Jordan," 9 March 1939, 334–35; "An Enemy of the People," 16 March 1939, 351; "Gas Light," 23 March 1939, 367; "To the Editor," 30 March 1939, 383–84; "The Family Reunion," 6 April 1939, 397–98; "Design for Living," 13 April 1939, 414–15; "Hampstead Heath," 20 April 1939, 10–11; "A Warrant from Nature," 27 April 1939, 23–24; "The Taming of the Shrew," 27 April 1939, 29; "The Women," 11 May 1939, 62–63; "The Intruder," 18 May 1939, 78–79; "Bridge Head," 25 May 1939, 95; "Crying in the Dark," 1 June 1939, 110–11; "Of Mice and Men," 8 June 1939, 126–27; "Rhondda Roundabout," 15 June 1939, 143; "Much Ado About Nothing," 22 June 1939, 159–160; "The Devil to Pay," 29 June 1939, 174–75; "A Mixed Bag," 6 July 1939, 190–91; "The Ellen Terry Barn Theatre," 13 July 1939, 207–8; "The Ascent of F6," 20 July 1939, 223–24; "The Gentle People," 27 July 1939, 238–39; "Night Without Tears," 19 October 1939, 11–12; "Our Village," 26 October 1939, 29–30; "To Sea in a Sieve," 16 November 1939, 75–76; "Music at Night," 20 November 1939, 102–3; "Caterwauling," 14 December 1939, 135–36; "Julius Caesar," 21 December 1939, 148–49; "Our Village II," 11 January 1940, 178–79; "Desire Under the Elms," 8 February 1940, 239–240; "The Importance of Being Earnest," 22 February 1940, 267–68; "Cousin Muriel," 28 March 1940, 340–41; "Three at a Time," 25 April 1940, 10–11; "The Light of Heart," 16 May 1940, 48–49; "Two at a Time," 30 May 1940, 73; 'Carried on to the Angel," 13 June 1940, 96–97; "Our Village III," 15 August 1940, 197–98; "Letters From Another World I, " 26 December 1940, 109; "Letters From Another World II," 2 January 1941, 125–26; "Letters From Another World III," 20 March 1941, 253–54; "Letters From Another World IV," 29 May 1941, 57–58; "Letters From Another World V," 28 August 1941, 184–85; "Letters From Another World VI," 4 December 1941, 56–57; "Letters From Another World VIII," 8 January 1942, 101–2; "Letters From Another World," 5 February 1942, 137–38; "Letters From Another World," 2 April 1942, 209–10; "Letters From Another World," 11 June 1942, 68–69; "Letters From Another World," 8 April 1943, 217–18; "Notes on a Homecoming," 27 September 1945, 177–79; "Children's Books," 20 December 1945, 97; "Hamlet, Lear, Macbeth, Wolfit," 4 April 1946, 245–46; "Red Rose and No Medals," 18 April 1946, 8–9; "The Movies," 30 May 1946, 69–70; "Portrait in Black: As You Like It: No Room at the Inn," 4 July 1946, 119–120; "The Castle of Perseverance,," 25 July 1946, 150; "Servant of Earth," 1 August 1946, 158–59; "A Diatribe," 17 October 1946, 8–9; "Arts Theatre

Club and The Garrick," 7 November 1946, 39–40; "The Winslow Boy and The Guinea Pig," 5 December 1946, 78–79; "Antony and Cleopatra and The Gleam," 9 January 1947, 123–24; "Message for Margaret and The Man from the Ministry," 6 February 1947, 162–63; "'The Living Stone,'" 6 March 1947, 179–80; "Born Yesterday and Jane," 20 March 1947, 202; "The Hidden Child," 10 April 1947, 225–27; "The White Devil," 24 April 1947, 18; "Candida and Now Barabbas," 8 May 1947, 35; "Call Home the Heart—St. James's Theatre," 22 May 1947, 54–55; "Richard II," 12 June 1947, 81–82; "Trespass: Globe Theatre," 18 September 1947, 171–72; "Ever Since Paradise and The Linden Tree," 2 October 1947, 190–91; "Musicals," 16 October 1947, 6–7; "You Never Can Tell and Operation Olivebranch," 30 October 1947, 27; "Fools," 13 November 1947, 45; "The Taming of the Shrew," 20 November 1947, 55; "Anna Lucasta: His Majesty's," 4 December 1947, 75; "Private Enterprise: St. James's and Dr. Angelus: Phoenix," 11 December 1947), 86–87; "Christmas and All That," 15 January 1948), 134–35; "Children's Books," 22 January 1948, 146–47; "St. Joan," 29 January 1948, 155; "Two Murderers," 5 February 1948, 165–66; "Gogol," 19 February 1948, 186–87; "Lyric, Hammersmith," 4 March 1948, 206; "Flagstad," 8 April 1948, 252–53; "Coriolanus," 22 April 1948, 18–19; "Curzon Cinema—Farrebique," 6 May 1948, 38–39; "Hamlet for Export," 3 June 1948, 81–82; "The Master Builder: Westminster," 17 June 1948, 106–7; "Yes Is for A Very Young Man—The Forty Eight Theatre and Corinth House—The New Lindsey Theatre," 1 July 1948, 129–130; "Crime Passionel: Lyric Theatre, Hammersmith," 15 July 1948, 152–53; "Twelfth Night: New Theatre," 30 September 1948, 238–39; "The Giaconda Smile: Wyndham's Theatre," 21 October 1948, 20–21; "Two Revivals," 11 November 1948, 56; "The Wild Duck," 25 November 1948, 81; "Children's Books," 2 December 1948, 94–95; "Grimm's," 9 December 1948, 103–4; "More Children's Books," 16 December 1948, 118; "The Cherry Orchard," 30 December 1948, 140–41; "The Return of the Prodigal," 3 February 1949, 201–2; "Richard III," 17 February 1949, 226–27; "The Heiress," 3 March 1949, 249; "By the Light of the Moon," 17 March 1949, 271–72; "The Human Touch," 31 March 1949, 297; "St. James's Theatre," 14 April 1949, 9–10; "Drama," 28 April 1949, 33; "'The Dream,'" 12 May 1949, 57; "The Lady's Not For Burning," 26 May 1949, 81; "Puppets," 9 June 1949, 105–6; "For Evans Sake," 23 June 1949, 130–31; "Love in Albania: Lyric, Hammersmith," 7 July 1949, 153–54; "A Ministry of Healing," 21 July 1949, 178–79; "Shaw," 28 July 1949, 189–190.

"Once I Saw a Fox Dancing Alone," *New York Herald Tribune Book Week,* 9 May 1965, 2, 26–27.

"Only Connect." In *Only Connect; Readings on Children's Literature.* edited by S. Egoff, G. T. Stubbs, L. F. Ashley. Toronto: Oxford University Press, 1969.

"On Not Writing for Children." *Children's Literature,* 4 (1975): 15–22.

In *Parabola: The Magazine of Myth and Tradition:* "The World of the Hero," 1.1 (1976): 42–47; "Two Pairs of Shoes," 1.3 (1976): 68–73; "The Once and Future Treasure," 1.3 (1976): 112–14; "Fear No More the Heat of the Sun," 2.1 (1977): 6–9; "The Legacy of the Ancestors," 2.2 (1977): 13–17; "If She's Not Gone, She Lives There Still," 3.1 (1978): 78–91; "Letter to a Learned Astrologer," 3.4 (1978): 58–65; "The Youngest Brother," 4.1 (1979): 38–43; "The Primary World," 4.3 (1979): 87–94; "Henny-Penny," 4.4 (1979): 79–80; "The Silk Drum," 5.2 (1980): 86–87; "Four Women," 5.4 (1980): 6–9; "What the Bees Know," 6.1 (1981): 42–50; "The Seventh Day," 7.1 (1982): 86–89; "Where Will All The Stories Go?," 7.2 (1982): 38–46; "Speak, Lord," 7.2 (1982): 80–86; "Name and No Name," 7.3 (1982): 42–46; "Leda's Lament," 7.4 (1982): 33–34; "Walking the Maze at Chartres," 8.1 (1983): 22–26; "A Parabola Bestiary," 8.2 (1983): 39–40; "What Aileth Thee?" 8.3 (1983): 16–17; "Re-storying the Adult," 8.4 (1983): 51–53; "Tarot Card No. 12 / The Hanged Man," 9.1 (1984): 47; "Miss Quigley," 9.2 (1984): 73–75; "The Way Back," 9.3 (1984): 60–63; "Sip No Sup and Bite No Bit," 9.4 (1984): 20–25; "Lucifer," 10.1 (1985): 92–93; "Now, Farewell and Hail," 10.2 (1985): 23–24; "On Unknowing," 10.3 (1985): 76–79; "The Garment," 10.4 (1985): 24–27; "The Unsleeping Eye: A Fairy Tale," 11.1 (1986): 19–22; "Nirvana is Samsara," 11.2 (1986): 30–31; "Out of Eden," 11.3 (1986): 16–17; "Lively Oracles," 11.4 (1986): 32–35; "Le Chevalier Perdu," 12.1 (1987): 14–17; "O Children of this World!," 12.2 (1987): 44–45; "On Forgiving Oneself," 12.3 (1987): 16–17; "Zen Moments," 12.4 (1987): 18–20; "The Interviewer," 13.1 (1988): 80–85; "Well, Shoot Me!" 13.2 (1988): 34–38; "Something Else," 13.3 (1988): 30–32; "Monte Perdido," 13.4 (1988): 19–21.

"Personal View." *Sunday Times,* 11 December 1988, G-4.

"A Radical Innocence." *New York Times Book Review,* 9 May 1965, 1, 38–39.

"Where Did She Come From? Why Did She Go?," *Saturday Evening Post,* 7 November 1964, 76–77.

"Who is Mary Poppins?," *Junior Bookshelf,* 18 (1954): 45–50.

"World Beyond World," *Chicago Sun-Times Book Week,* 7 May 1967, 4–5.

Secondary Sources

1. Books and Surveys

Bergsten, Staffan. *Mary Poppins and Myth*. Stockholm: Almquist & Wiksell, 1978. Examines the first four books in light of mythic and epic motifs of ascent, descent, and creation.

Cameron, Eleanor. *The Green and Burning Tree; On the Writing and Enjoyment of Children's Books*. Boston: Little, Brown and Company, 1962. Questions Travers' dissatisfaction with the idea of writing for children and charges that Travers has presented an erroneous impression of Beatrix Potter's motives.

Carpenter, Humphrey and Mari Prichard. *The Oxford Companion to Children's Literature*. New York: Oxford University Press, 1984. Concludes that the magic is used arbitrarily and that the stories are disjointed.

Commire, Anne, ed. *Something About the Author*. Vol. 54. Detroit: Gale Research, 1989. Provides the most extensive survey of Travers' career.

Cott, Jonathan. *Pipers at the Gates of Dawn; The Wisdom of Children's Literature*. New York: Random House, 1983. Contains the most in-depth published interview with Travers, in which she discusses the influences of Zen and mystic texts.

Eyre, Frank. *British Children's Books in the Twentieth Century*. London: Longman, 1971. Labels Mary Poppins a magical personality whose Olympian authority corresponds to the way nannies appear to children.

Gathorne-Hardy, Jonathan. *The Unnatural History of the Nanny*. New York: Dial Press, 1973. Charts the popularity of this figure over a ninety-year period and adduces evidence, from literature and life, about her roles as nurse, mother substitute, and, occasionally, sexual temptress and initiator.

Green, Roger Lancelyn. *Tellers of Tales; Children's Books and Their Authors from 1800 to 1968*. London: Kaye & Ward, 1969. Applauds the Poppins books for capturing the child's fantasy world, in which nothing is impossible.

Hendrickson, Linnea. *Children's Literature: A Guide to the Criticism*. Boston: G. K. Hall, 1987. Summarizes briefly most of the available Travers criticism.

Lynn, Ruth. *Fantasy for Children; An Annotated Checklist and Reference Guide*. 2d ed. New York: R. R. Bowker, 1983. Lists only six of the Poppins books and a smattering of reviews.

Newquist, Roy. *Conversations*. Chicago: Rand McNally & Co., 1967. Interviews Travers mainly on the subjects of her family and school life in Australia.

Reckford, Kenneth J. *Aristophanes' Old-and-New Comedy*. Chapel Hill: The University of North Carolina Press, 1987. Establishes the Mary Poppins stories as Dionysian fairy tales, against which to measure Aristophanes' comedies.

Riley, Carolyn, ed. *Children's Literature Review*. Vol. 2. Detroit: Gale Research, 1976. Samples reviews of Travers' work.

Townsend, John Rowe. *Written for Children; An Outline of English-language Children's Literature*. London: Garnet Miller, 1965. Speculates that Mary Poppins' American popularity may be due to the books' illusions about English domestic life.

2. Articles, Reviews, and Interviews

Bart, Peter and Dorothy. "As Told and Sold by Disney." *New York Times Book Review*, 9 May 1965, 2, 32–34. Laments the spell that money and gimmickry have always exerted over Walt Disney.

Burness, Edwina and Griswold, Jerry. "The Art of Fiction LXXIII: P. L. Travers." *Paris Review* 86 (1982): 210–29. Travers describes her process of writing as one of listening.

Carpenter, Humphrey. "Mary Poppins, Force of Nature." *New York Times Book Review*, 27 August 1989, 29. Characterizes Mary Poppins as an Australian's imagining of a very English childhood and discounts *MPHND* as slight and skimpy.

Cary, Joseph. "Six Beauties Sleeping." *Children's Literature* 6 (1977): 224–34. Praises *About the Sleeping Beauty* as one of Travers' premier creations.

Cott, Jonathan. "About the Sleeping Beauty." *New York Times Book Review*, 28 September 1975, 27–28. Credits the extraordinary and soulful insights of the afterword.

Field, Michele. "Reminiscing with P. L. Travers." *Publishers Weekly*, 21 March 1986, 40–41. Travers speaks about her various jobs before coming to England.

Graham, Janet. "The Cup of Sorrow in Every Woman's Life." *Ladies' Home Journal* 84. no. 2 (1967): 68–70. Travers talks obliquely of sorrow in her own life.

Hearn, Michael Patrick. "P. L. Travers in Fantasy Land." *Children's Literature* 6 (1977): 221–24. Expresses disappointment in the anticlimactic and protracted retelling of Sleeping Beauty.

Heins, Paul. "P. L. Travers, *Friend Monkey*." *Horn Book* 48 (1972): 53–54. Criticizes the story as ludicrous without being funny.

Hoffeld, Laura. "Where Magic Begins." *The Lion and the Unicorn* 3, no. 1 (1979): 4–13. Characterizes all adults in the Mary Poppins books, except the heroine, as Dagwood Bumsteads.

Lingeman, Richard R. "Visit with Mary Poppins and P. L. Travers." *New York Times Magazine,* 25 December 1966, 12–13, 27–29. Travers mentions childhood amusements and memories.

Moore, Anne Carroll. "Mary Poppins." *Horn Book* 11 (January–February 1935): 6–7. Welcomes the book as a major work by an author worth watching.

Moore, Robert B. "A Letter from a Critic." *Children's Literature* 10 (1982): 211–13. Questions the effects of the original "Bad Tuesday" chapter on the child's self-image and image of others.

Nodelman, Perry. "Introduction: On Words and Pictures, Neglected Noteworthies, and Touchstones in Training," in *Touchstones: Reflections on the Best in Children's Literature,* vol. 3, edited by P. Nodelman. Purdue University: Children's Literature Association, 1989. Charges that, despite Travers' insistent advertising, neither Poppins nor her fantasy is engaging.

Philip, Neil. "The Writer and the Nanny Who Never Explain." *Times Educational Supplement,* 11 June 1982, 42. Travers reiterates her stand on the pointlessness of biographical data and explanations.

Roddy, Joseph. "A Visit with the Real Mary Poppins." *Look,* 13 December 1966, 84–6. Travers talks about the experience of living at Smith College.

Schwartz, Albert V. "*Mary Poppins* Revised: An Interview with P. L. Travers." *Interracial Books for Children Bulletin* 5 no. 3 (1974): 1–5. Cites extracts from many of Travers' books to prove racist bias; Travers questions the overemphasis and contends that racism is foreign to her.

Smith, Rosemary. "Walt Disney's *Mary Poppins*." *Elementary English* 44 (January 1967): 29–31. Charges that Disney has limited the scope and ruined the quality of Mary Poppins' magic.

Yolen, Jane. "Makers of Modern Myths." *Horn Book* 51 (1975): 496–7. Claims Travers as a mythmaker who writes for the child as believer.

Ziner, Feenie. "Mary Poppins as a Zen Monk." *New York Times Book Review,* 7 May 1972, 2. Draws the parallel with Zen because Mary Poppins always contains a secret.

3. Miscellaneous

AE. *An Essay on the Character in Irish Literature*. Dublin: Cuala Press, 1932.

———. *The Hero in Man*. London: Orpheus Press, 1909.

———. *Selected Poems*. London: Macmillan, 1935.

Benstock, Shari, ed. *Feminist Issues in Literary Scholarship*. Bloomington: Indiana University Press, 1987.

Brady, Jim. "Mother Goose Plucked Clean." *The Globe and Mail,* 21 January 1989, C-1.

Dürckheim, Karlfried Graf. "The Call for the Master." *Parabola* 14 no. 2 (1989): 4–13.

———. *The Japanese Cult of Tranquility,* translated by Eda O'Shiel. London: Rider & Co., 1960.

Farrow, George Edward. *The Wallypug of Why*. London: Hutchinson, 1895.

Hennecke, E. and Schneemelcher, W., eds. *New Testament Apocrypha*. 2 vols. London: Lutterworth, 1965.

Irvine, Louise. *Royal Doulton Series Ware*. 3 vols. London: Richard Dennis, 1986.

Kristeva, Julia. *Desire in Language; A Semiotic Approach to Literature and Art,* translated by T. Gora, A. Jardine, L. S. Roudiez. New York: Columbia University Press, 1980.

Masefield, John. *The Box of Delights*. London: Heinemann, 1935.

———. *The Midnight Folk*. London: Heinemann, 1927.

Opie, Iona and Peter, eds. *The Oxford Dictionary of Nursery Rhymes*. Oxford: At the Clarendon Press, 1952.

Sartre, Jean-Paul. *Search for a Method*. New York: Knopf, 1967.

Waugh, Evelyn. *A Handful of Dust*. London: Chapman & Hall, 1934.

Woolf, Virginia. *The Pargiters,* edited by Mitchell Leaska. London: The Hogarth Press, 1978.

Index

The Author

Patricia Demers is professor of English at the University of Alberta, where she teaches courses in Renaissance and children's literature. She has edited two anthologies of children's literature for Oxford University Press, *From Instruction to Delight* (with R. G. Moyles) and *A Garland from the Golden Age,* and has published articles on George Chapman, Francis Bacon, Richard Crashaw, and emblem books. She is now at work on a study of women's contributions to the tradition of biblical interpretation.